CALLING ON FIRE

Ashley Boggan and Chris Heckert

CALLING ON FIRE

Reclaiming the Method of Methodism

Nashville

CALLING ON FIRE:
RECLAIMING THE METHOD OF METHODISM

Copyright© 2025 by Abingdon Press

All rights reserved.

No part of this work may be reproduced or transmitted in any form or by any means, electronic or mechanical, including photocopying and recording, or by any information storage or retrieval system, except as may be expressly permitted by the 1976 Copyright Act, the 1998 Digital Millennium Copyright Act, or in writing from the publisher. Requests for permission should be addressed to Permissions, Abingdon Press, 810 12th Avenue South, Nashville, TN 37203-4704, or emailed to permissions@abingdonpress.com.

ISBN: 9781791037185

Library of Congress Control Number has been requested.

Scripture quotations unless noted otherwise are from the Common English Bible. Copyright © 2011 by the Common English Bible. All rights reserved. Used by permission. www.CommonEnglishBible.com.

MANUFACTURED IN THE UNITED STATES OF AMERICA

CONTENTS

Introduction	vii
Field Preaching	1
Micro-Communities	25
Social Engagement	49
Leadership Activation	73
Conclusion	99

INTRODUCTION

"Tradition is not the worship of ashes, but the preservation of fire." —*Gustav Mahler*

It all started in Bristol...

There was something about looking out at the seasoned wood of the pulpit, altar rail, and floorboards as we listened to our host reading old words from a journal. We had come from all over, in the United States and a few other countries to participate in a sacred pilgrimage to (re)discover the roots of Methodism. At that particular moment we were sitting in John Wesley's New Room in Bristol, UK, where then-director of global relationships David Worthington read an entry from Wesley's journal dated April 2, 1739.

> At four in the afternoon, I submitted to be more vile and proclaimed in the highways the glad tidings of salvation, speaking from a little eminence in a ground adjoining to the city, to about three thousand people. The Scripture on which I spoke was this: "The Spirit of the Lord is upon me, because he hath anointed me to preach the gospel to the poor; he hath sent me to heal the broken-hearted, to preach deliverance to the captives, and recovering of sight to the blind, to set at liberty them that are bruised, to proclaim the acceptable year of the Lord."[1]

Both the words we heard and the wood beams holding up the room were birthed in the same era. The construction of the New Room was

Introduction

a direct result of Wesley's decision to take the risk of being vile, preaching out in the field for the first time. He would eventually walk on those floors, preach from that pulpit, and serve at that communion rail. But it was something more that helped those words come to life in a new way and resonate with power and conviction.

The two of us (Chris and Ashley) met on that pilgrimage and sat together with the group in the New Room feeling similar sentiments. Back home, something wasn't working. The COVID-19 pandemic was fading but the church seemed forever changed. Infighting over human sexuality was fueling imminent division. Years of avoiding in-person gatherings had made many church members reluctant to return to worship. Numbers were down in nearly every measurable category. Agencies and conferences were trying to prepare for the long-term effects of decline and trying to chart a sustainable course in the new normal. Any high-level connectional conversation seemed to focus on a shared budget that was described as a "shrinking pie," the death/decline of the church membership, and pitted the general agencies against bishops in terms of who uses (implied in conversations as "wastes") more resources. Church, as we had known it, was forever changed. We had come on pilgrimage for renewal and perhaps to find a little hope for the long journey ahead.

"Submitted to be more vile" rang with both a sense of defeat and hope that resonated with our own realities. A person *submits* when they no longer want to fight against the inevitable. It's often seen as a negative or dehumanizing act. But there is also beauty in submitting to something and no longer resisting a greater force that can birth new possibilities. To us, the word *vile* caught us off guard and was fresh and radical enough to mirror our own willingness to try something new, regardless of how crazy, uncouth, or unconventional it might be. If we submitted to be more vile might it restore joy and hope for the future of United Methodism?

Even though both of us studied the history of early Methodism, and were not unfamiliar with Wesley's episode in Bristol, visiting the New Room in a season of burnout and worry imbued a spirit of willful creativity to unearth and explore how Wesley's submission to the vile changed the course of Methodism and even the world. Perhaps if submitting to the previously unthinkable could forge a new path in the eighteenth century, the same spirit of willingness could open a new door for followers of Jesus in the twenty-first century.

During that pilgrimage we formed both a friendship and a partnership in seeking to do something with the shared discovery from Bristol. We wanted to do as Wesley did, try new things, adapt, and multiply what worked for the sake of the church's mission. I (Ashley) would go on to develop talks and presentations for the United Methodist Council of Bishops, annual conferences, and seminaries on the call to "Be more vile" and the need to focus less on congregational vitality and more on "Wesleyan *vile*-tality" which I began to define as:

> a willingness to look beyond today's acceptable practices, standards, and norms and bend the rules in order to ensure that more and more persons can be included within the Kin-dom of God. And also, that all persons, no matter who they are, how they identify, whom they love, or how they live can know and experience the love of God, can know their own self-worth, and can grow to love themselves and so that they can love others.[2]

While I (Chris) would begin doctoral studies at Wesley House in Cambridge, UK, in partnership with Wesley Seminary in DC, particularly studying "Compassion, Justice, and Witness: Ministry in Turbulent Times," both of our endeavors continued the trajectory begun together in Bristol: to explore what it means to submit to be more vile today for the sake of fulfilling the church's primary mission. Ashley's path would lead her to author the book *Wesleyan Vile-tality: Reclaiming the Heart of Methodist Identity* (a book that works well in conjunction with this one), and Chris would pilot a project for his doctorate of ministry program that has served as the basis for much of the practical theory presented in this book. We both set out to discern *vile*-tality in our ministries, and would realize that this might just be at the heart of Methodism. But questions still lingered: How do you embody *vile*-tality? How did Wesley embody *vile*-tality? What did Wesley do that we aren't? What did he do that we can no longer do and what might we be able to reclaim? Over

Introduction

time, we realized that the answer to these questions lies in identifying and reclaiming the "method" of Methodism.

This book proposes a way forward for The United Methodist Church through a reclaiming of our original methodology. By examining four core practices that fueled early Methodism, we offer both historical insights and practical applications to help contemporary churches recover their missional effectiveness in today's challenging landscape.

The Practical Wesleyan Quadrilateral

Much like Albert Outler in the 1960s created the "Wesleyan Quadrilateral" (Scripture, tradition, reason, and experience) to assist United Methodists with reclaiming Wesleyan theology, we are using hindsight to recreate Wesley's method of Methodism, which we are calling "The Practical Wesleyan Quadrilateral" (or simply "the Practical Quad" throughout this book). To develop the Practical Quad, we looked at John Wesley's ministry over the entirety of his life. We examined tracts, journals, sermons, hymns, and actions of John and early Methodists to look for things that were most consistent across time, place, and space. The method that we lay out in this book was not a chronological development of Wesley's. And John Wesley never stated or even implied that his "method" was fourfold nor contained these components. You will notice (or at least we hope you do) that many of these components developed in or from the town of Bristol. We don't believe this is mere coincidence. As we both experienced firsthand, there's something about Bristol that calls one back to our roots; and we think there was something about Bristol that called Wesley out.

The Practical Quad we propose in this book is, aptly, fourfold: field preaching, micro-communities, social engagement, and leadership activation. We define each of these and elaborate on their origin, their embodiment, and their connection to and potential for changed ministry today in the following chapters.

Introduction

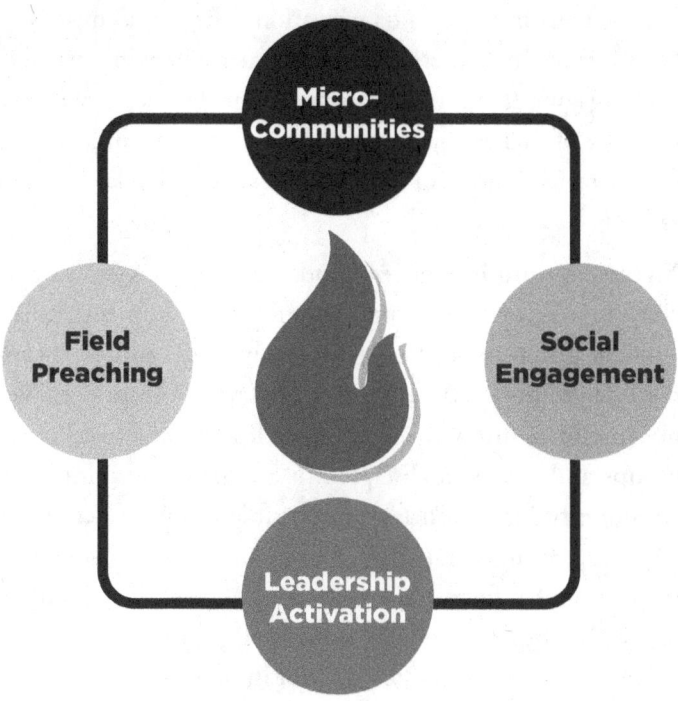

Let's break down the Quad:

1. **Field preaching**, as a concept, is not going literally into the fields to preach, but is instead taking the message of God's love outside the walls of the church to where people are gathered. The types of field preaching in today's context involve various types of media, community engagement, and spaces. We might think of modern field preaching as a form of content creation. What is the message that others need to hear that they either are not hearing inside the church or will not enter the church building to hear? There is a wide variety of content out there, and people often specialize in one media or another. After all, a running joke is that most people have a podcast (or two or three). Field preaching or content creation can include preaching, blogging, social media influencing, Fresh Expressions ministries, podcasting, or simply meeting people and

Introduction

talking faith in a casual conversation. The main emphasis behind it is having a message that is actually drawing listeners in and engaging them in a meaningful way. For us, as Wesleyans, the crux of that message must be God's all-encompassing love for *all* of us which compels us to live out our faith through radical acts of love.

2. **Micro-communities** are our updated term for Wesley's bands, classes, and societies. Some congregations and leaders excel at small group work, but small group work and/or covenant disciple groups are different from micro-communities. We do not intend to throw shade on those leaders who excel at small groups and covenant discipleship groups because intentional community formation feels impossible as our society has become increasingly transient. As we constantly move, we have to form and reform new connections, new relationships, all of which requires a level of vulnerability that is rare. Furthermore, coming together (virtually or in person) is also less common today. There's a running joke in #momlife that if you want to plan a get-together with other moms you'll need to book six months out. In my (Ashley's) experience, this is less of a joke and more of a sad reality. We are all constantly pulled in so many directions and have to wear so many different hats, that in all honesty, at the end of the day, do I want to open up and bear my soul to other people? Not really. But, as I've seen by implementing intentional small group relationships, it's actually quite beautiful and relieving to know that we're all struggling a whole lot right now (and many of us in similar ways), and that there are others who are committed to holding us up and watching over us in love.

3. **Social engagement** centers around the fact that one of the core aspects of Wesley's belief was the interconnectedness of personal holiness (one's own relationship with God) and social holiness (one's relationship with neighbor). For Wesley, the two were interdependent. You could not love God *without* lov-

Introduction

ing neighbor. And loving God and neighbor were not passive forms of love; they were active! The crux of the Methodist faith is: *faith acted out as love*. The way that Wesley embodied love was primarily through social engagement. Most Methodists of the eighteenth century were classified as impoverished. Wesley sought to better their lives through systemic change and addressing stated needs. Today, we are too often engaging socially in ways that are comfortable for us. We write checks—and yes, money is definitely still needed for mission—and we assemble flood buckets for UMCOR, we host a canned food or a coat drive, maybe we even sponsor a soup kitchen once in a while. All of these forms of social engagement, however, are comfortable for us. They do not force us out into the community, among those in need, building relationships across boundaries, and responding collectively to need. This is the type of social engagement Wesley called for. He went to where people were and asked them what they needed, and then he provided it; and he kept doing this over and over and over again. As needs adapted and changed, so did his response. Today, we cannot keep doing mission or social engagement in the same way we did thirty or forty years ago or taking the same missiology to different communities, assuming that what worked in one space will work in another.

4. **Leadership activation** is the empowerment of all persons, according to their gifts and graces, to lead in creative ways to keep United Methodism moving. Wesley encouraged persons to not simply *do*, but to *lead*. The reason that his method was readily replicable is because it was simple, designed to multiply, and open to mutation. As persons moved, as needs changed, Wesley recognized that some persons might be better suited than others (and occasionally even better than himself) for leadership in specific communities or spaces. As needs arose, as persons stated that they were burned-out or uncomfortable leading in a certain way, Wesley responded. He kept adapting

and creating new roles for people to occupy. Most importantly, Wesley delegated! Yes, Wesley was a bit of a control freak and a mild ego-maniac but he was also someone who offered constant opportunities for those whom society had silenced to speak up and out. And Wesley looked for the moving Spirit of God in people whom society had cast aside; he gave these persons a preferential place to lead and have a voice. How do we better do this type of leadership activation today?

It cannot be stated enough that the proposed Practical Quad is a method, not a menu. In order for the Practical Quad to work, all of it must be implemented. Yes, we know that some congregations are already really good at social engagement or at field preaching. However, are they truly embodying the Practical Quad of Methodism if they are not connecting these attributes to micro-communities and leadership activation? We would argue, no.

A quite curious aspect of this proposed Practical Quad is that very little of it was of Wesley's own mind. Much like his theology, Wesley borrowed ideas, tools, thoughts, sayings, structures, etc. from those around him. He saw what worked in other spaces and adapted it to work within his contexts for the Methodists. He borrowed the theological doctrine of assurance as well as the micro-community "bands" from the Moravians. He learned of new forms of social engagement from persons like William Morgan, who first suggested doing ministry in the Oxford prisons. He even followed his own mother's suggestion that the Spirit of God can speak through laypersons, too, encouraging Wesley to activate new leaders. What made John Wesley almost an ecclesiological genius was taking these seemingly disconnected ideas and structures and organizing them into an effective and efficient missional system that engaged all persons within all levels of society to embody the love of God through action. This is the method, the Practical Quad, that we'll lay out for you over these chapters. And this is the way that we, as United Methodists, could once again embody or deploy in order to grow God's love in this world and to live into our mission of making disciples of Jesus Christ for the transformation of the world.

Introduction

Before we turn you over to the components of the method before us, a note on voice. We've written this book seeking to maintain our two voices while also being comfortable using "I" throughout. Most of the following chapters begin with Rev. Dr. Chris Heckert summarizing the problem of the day. Then Dr. Ashley Boggan steps in to provide the historic context for how Wesley addressed the problem and the development of that particular component of the method. Chris wraps it up by examining how the historic Wesleyan method could be implemented today and provides practical resources. There are times where we've overlapped our voices. Perhaps most importantly—we didn't want this to be another book without practical applications, and so each chapter ends with resources ready for your use to assist you in deploying the Practical Quad. However, to tease you a bit . . .

Why Is a Practical Quad Necessary?

Simply, and perhaps boldly, stated: **The United Methodist Church has a mission, but not a method.**

The United Methodist Church's stated mission is: To make disciples of Jesus Christ for the transformation of the world. This is a noble mission rooted both in Scripture and Wesleyan theology. The deeper question, however, is how do we live into this mission? How do we make disciples? Also, what exactly is a disciple? How do they act in the world? While we are at it, what sort of world transformation are we working toward and how do we measure or know if we've achieved it? The reality is that while The UMC has incredible leaders and congregations, we find ourselves in this new era with a mission without a method. Thus, a Practical Quad is necessary.

If we were to diagnose the issue that isn't working within United Methodism (and perhaps in most organized religions) it would be much more significant than simply institutional decline. The greater issue that fuels worry, burnout, and conflict is not having a common sense of purpose. Why are we doing this? Is it to save aging buildings? Are we trying to preserve traditions, programs, and structures from a bygone era? Is it out of habit or fear of irrelevance? Perhaps there is a uniting vision that can renew both energy and vision for those who seek to make a difference in people's lives.

Today, so many preachers are burned out. The pandemic has seemingly quadrupled pressure on ministers as in-person and virtual worship are now expected. Persons are still in crisis and seeking to recover from the physical, familiar, communal, emotional, and spiritual loss of the last few years. Pastors today are also asked to preach in an incredibly sensitive yet politically charged time. And budgets—don't get me started on declining church budgets; it's a problem that I'm sure we all know about. Persons in the pews attend church on Sunday mornings when their kids' soccer schedules allow, and they have great visions for what they want their churches to do. However, when it comes to implementing those visions, few people seem to have the time, gumption, or energy to do so. As Michael Beck has brilliantly pointed out, we are increasingly entering an epidemic of loneliness. Lessons we can learn from the past inform us that this is not the first time any of this has happened. Churches have declined because of a lack of institutional grit. People have been over-extended and under-appreciated. Clergy have been exhausted by their calls and overwhelmed by their tasks. All of this was also going on when Methodism first began in the eighteenth century, and it's in answering these questions or addressing these problems that the original movement of the people called Methodists offered support to a tired, shrinking, static church. Today, we should take a lesson from our past and reengage the Practical Quad that John Wesley laid out for us over three hundred years ago. If we intentionally nurture disciples of Jesus Christ through this fourfold method, perhaps persons will find a renewed, reinvigorated, reclaimed purpose of faith acted out as love.

A Light Refresher on Methodist Origins

What's in a name? Many are curious about the etymology of their own names. I was named "Ashley" after the flower girl at my parents' wedding.

Introduction

And the name itself means "a field of ash trees." (Ironically, I'm deathly allergic to ash trees.) Our names often carry assumptions, most of them dictating a social trend of a period of our lives. Similarly, the name or label "Methodist" carried many assumptions in eighteenth-century England—and most of them were not positive.

For those of you who are new to Methodism or are wondering why we should care about a dead, white Oxford don, here's some context. John Wesley was the son of an ordained minister in the Church of England (Samuel Wesley), and did his best to live up to his mother's (Susanna Annesley Wesley) claim that he was a "brand plucked from the burning." (Backstory: there was a fire at the Epworth rectory when John was five years old and he was saved at the very last minute, prompting his mother to refer to him as a "brand plucked from the burning.") And while John followed somewhat in his dad's footsteps, he didn't want to be a parish priest; he felt called to do something more (probably because his mother repeatedly told him that he was saved for something special and his father was openly despised by his parish).

The movement of the people called Methodist began in the late 1720s when Charles Wesley began a religious society on the campus of Oxford University—a group of which his brother John quickly assumed control. The group became quickly known for their "weird" ways of "doing" religion. They engaged in acts of piety on a regular basis—generally not the norm at the time. They rose early, prayed regularly, studied Scripture, fasted weekly, and talked openly with one another about their spiritual condition. Within a few months, they would add works of mercy to their spiritual practice, actively engaging with the community, particularly those outcast, in an affirming, empowering way that genuinely upset the status quo.

Many assume that the etymology of "Methodist" comes from the routinized acts of personal piety performed by those early Oxford-ites, often called "the Holy Club." Or even from Susanna Wesley's strict childcare routine. The term "Methodist" was originally a derogatory label not preferred by John Wesley. (In his 1742 treatise *The Character of a Methodist*, he wrote, "I would rejoice . . . if the name [Methodist] were buried

Introduction

in eternal oblivion and mentioned never again." Sorry, John—it stuck.) "Methodist" was also a term used widely by the mid-eighteenth century to include those even outside of Wesley's movement. As historian Ryan Danker claims, "The term 'Methodist' was often attached to those with no association to the movement's leaders; instead, it was used as a term of derision for those with evangelical or irregular tendencies, actions bathed in volatile political and social meaning."[3]

While many assume that this term was used to describe the methodical spiritual disciplines that the Wesleys' Oxford club followed, it wasn't until their faith began to be acted out in acts of mercy that they began to be called more than the "Holy Club."

Under the suggestion of Holy Clubber William Morgan, they began visiting those imprisoned at the Bocardo and the Castle, just outside Oxford. Their ministries with those most outcast—the imprisoned—earned them a raging letter to the editor in the *Fog's Weekly Journal* of 1732, a popular Oxford newspaper. This letter described the Holy Club as "sons of sorrow," "shameless gutgazers," "madmen and fools." Despite the various epithets thrown against this group in this article, the name that began to stick was "this sect called Methodist." This article is the first time that the word *Methodist* is printed in association with the Wesley brothers and their Oxford society. Its author went on to criticize their theology and their practices. It seems, however, that the letter is written because this group was beginning to cause "no small stir in Oxford." Suddenly this group was doing something new—and that new thing wasn't their personal acts of piety. The new thing they were doing was prison ministry.

In their day, Oxford University was literally walled off from the surrounding countryside. It was believed by those who attended or worked for the university that this literal wall kept them safe from the rugged countrypeople perceived to be illiterate, dirty, and immoral. The prisons for the county were also directly along or outside the city walls. It's with these prisons in sight that John Wesley—under the prompting of William Morgan—breaches the literal, physical wall of Oxford and begins prison ministry.

Introduction

One inmate in particular began to pluck John Wesley's not-yet-strangely-warmed heartstrings. His name was Thomas Blair, and he was imprisoned on the alleged crime of "sodomitical practices." Wesley's ministry with Blair has long been known and documented in both primary and secondary sources (but has rarely been talked about openly today).[4] Wesley wrote in his journal and diary more about Blair than any other inmate, and Wesley took a special interest in Blair's legal case, even going so far as to intervene for him and attend his trial. How this relates to the name "Methodist" is that the letter in the *Fog's Weekly Journal* that accuses them of "no small stir" is alluding to Wesley's prison ministry, specifically his ministry with Blair.

With this singular act of mercy, those associated with the Holy Club took one literal step too far. They went from being "tolerated" to "castigated."[5] For many, their breaching the physical walls of the city began to tear down the metaphorical walls that kept the elite "safe" (or at least separate) from the illiterate and kept the free person separate from the imprisoned. According to Methodist historian Richard Heitzenrater, at Oxford, "[The Methodists] expended more energy in acts of social concern throughout the city than in acts of corporate devotion within the walls of the university."[6] By going to where the poor and imprisoned were, John Wesley and the Holy Club transgressed the social and religious understandings of those who were deemed worthy of the message of God's love. Grounding our name in this story means that we are called Methodist because of how we take the love of God to unforeseen places—to the outcast, the imprisoned, the silenced.

It's in Oxford where John and his friends begin to lay the foundation for the Practical Quad, but it is not in Oxford where the Practical Quad is fully laid out. The full Practical Quad would develop over decades of responding innovatively to problems that arose along the way.

From Oxford, the Methodists ventured outward. Some took preaching positions at local parishes; others, like the Wesley brothers, would try on a missionary hat for a few years. They all converged back in London in 1738. It's in this year that Charles first feels a "strange palpitation of the heart" on May 21 and John feels a "strangely warmed heart" three days later, May 24, 1738. In London, they led a religious society known as the Fetterlane Society and continued to fine-tune a more practical form of Christian living. However, it wasn't until John was called to Bristol in March 1739 that the method or Practical Quad of Methodism really began to take shape. And it's in Bristol where the story of Methodism and the story that opened this book begin.

Calling on Fire

As the twentieth century composer Gustav Mahler aptly stated, "Tradition is not the worship of ashes, but the preservation of fire." A more accurate translation of the original German would be to "pass on the flame," indicating transmission into a new vessel. Our delving into history is not for the purpose of elevating, or worshipping the past, but rather to transmit the fire of our movement into the present—not to preserve fire, but to allow the same fire to burn anew. Fire cannot burn through the same piece of wood twice, but must burn new wood, or whatever material would be consumed by the flame. We are grateful for the spirit fire that blazed through the witness of our spiritual forebears, but we know that the same passion and world-transforming flame that once brought about revival might spread again as we harness the methods of connecting the different components of Wesley's practical quad together.

When building a fire, it is important to start with light, dry wood that will burn quickly. Once the kindling catches fire you can add more substantial wood. It is important, however to avoid putting on wood that is too heavy or too wet, otherwise, it will put out the flame. Once the fire is burning hot enough it can take heavier and wetter wood. This is how the Practical Quad works and how we hope this book may work within our modern Methodist movement. We begin with a spark that ignites interest and hope through field preaching, adding micro communities that help the fire to build in strength and heat, spreading the flames through social engagement, and ultimately transmitting the flame to bring light and heat to new places through leadership activation. By reclaiming this method of Methodism, we are calling on fire—an ancient flame that has not died out and is ready to be passed along so that new generations might enjoy its heat.

As we begin to build the fire together, let's delve into the Practical Quad.

Notes

1. John Wesley, "Entry April 2nd, 1739," in *The Journal of John Wesley*, ed. Nehemiah Curnock, vol. II (Epworth Press, 1911), 172–73.
2. Ashley Boggan, *Wesleyan Vile-tality: Reclaiming the Heart of Wesleyan Identity* (Abingdon Press, 2025).
3. Ryan Danker, *Wesley and the Anglicans* (IVP Academic, 2016), 15.
4. V. H. H. Green, *The Young Mr. Wesley* (Wyvern Books, 1963); Richard Heitzenrater, *Mirror and Memory: Reflections on Early Methodism* (Kingswood Books, 1989); and Henry Abelove, *The Evangelist of Desire: John Wesley and the Methodists* (Stanford University Press, 1990).
5. Peter Forsaith, "'too indelicate to mention . . .': Transgressive Male Sexualities in Early Methodism," *Methodist Review* 12 (2020): 61–84.
6. Heitzenrater, *Mirror and Memory*, 64–65.

FIELD PREACHING

"Hey, have you subscribed to my podcast yet?"

"There is a glorious door opened among the colliers. You must come and water what God has enabled me to plant." —George Whitefield, March 3, 1739[1]

"It struck into my mind, 'Leave off preaching. How can you preach to others, who have not faith yourself?... [But Bohler] said 'Preach faith till you have it; and then, because you have it, you will preach faith." —John Wesley, 1738[2]

> **Field Preaching**—a message of God's love taken outside the walls of the church to those who are most vulnerable, most outcast, and most in need of affirmation.

As we unpack the elements of the Practical Quad, we begin with John Wesley's decision to "be more vile" and give in to the practice of field preaching. While he was reluctant to proclaim the gospel in such an unconventional way, he ultimately chose to do what was necessary to meet people where they were so they would receive a message they needed to hear, a message of God's liberating love. The same crowds of people would never have gone inside of a church to hear him or any other preacher preach a sermon. Field preaching would become a hallmark of Methodism as it spread throughout England and beyond, often at the condemnation of the established church.

Today we see field preaching as not just preaching a sermon in an open field or public square, but any act of proclamation that meets people where they are for the sake of offering a message of God's liberating love. In a digital world the field can be found in online and virtual spaces, as well as physical places like cafes, rehab centers, and tattoo parlors. Moving proclamation outside of church walls can feel as uncouth today as it did in Wesley's day. But just as the church in his time was struggling to meet people who needed a message of hope and love the most, we are at a point where submitting to be more vile for the sake of the church's mission no longer feels like an option. We have this message in jars of clay, so we must use whatever means we have to share it so that those who struggle, those who are alone, those who suffer from oppression and injustice might find renewed life. So, what does it mean for us to submit to be more vile today?

The Problem Today

On a youth group retreat to a local camp, I watched a movie called *Field of Dreams*. A mantra from that movie is whispered to the character played by Kevin Costner, Ray Kinsella, as he is walking through a cornfield, "If you build it, they will come." That movie quickly became a favorite of some of our youth leaders. For decades I would hear this phrase in the context of church ministry, "If you build it, they will come." While in certain seasons, this idea may have been true, it is no longer a helpful narrative in the church. We have the buildings, so why won't they just come?

If we could just get more people to come, more younger people, we could turn things around. Many UM churches have signs or slogans that proclaim "Open Hearts, Open Minds, Open Doors." Our doors are open to all! Come on in! You are welcome here!

This is the longing for every church I have visited or pastored. We long for a time when pews were full, choirs were robust, budgets were adequate, and our fellowship halls were bursting with life. The reality today is that of roughly 30,000 United Methodist churches in the US, a majority of those congregations likely have few than 25 people in weekly worship. In 2019, over 65% of all UMCs had an average weekly worship attendance of fewer than 50 people.[3]

So all we need to do is get more people to come inside on Sunday mornings, right?

Perhaps we are trying to solve the wrong problem, or at least we are not addressing the root of it. Today, people of all classes, ethnicities, identities, and segments of society are grappling with real issues, and yet people are disconnected and isolated. In 2023, the Surgeon General of the United States Dr. Vivek Murthy, released a report titled "Our Epidemic of Loneliness and Isolation," in which he identifies trending asocial and antisocial behaviors that have become endemic in our society to the point of being a public health concern.[4] The pervasiveness of social media and the use of technology as a primary medium to interact with others, along with a decrease of civic participation including religious communities, has caused an increase of social anxiety and mental health problems stemming from feelings of loneliness and isolation.

A 2019 research study conducted by Sara Konrath at Indiana University sought to test a 2009 study of college students that reported a significant decrease of empathy among young adults over a period of 30 years. Konrath's research confirmed the trending decline in empathy among college students but also noted a correlating trend. While students' ability to feel or express empathy for others decreased, a corresponding increase in narcissism and narcissistic behaviors was documented. She identified social media ("Did you like my reel?") and technological use ("I'm trending! #blessed") as primary culprits of younger adults not developing the same social skills and ability to express compassion for others in the ways that previous generations have, and in the ways that church has commonly (or "traditionally") taught.

Today there are other real issues that people are experiencing, including poverty, economic challenges, rampant racism and discrimination, along with physical and mental health concerns, as well as a genuine fear for (maybe even of) the future. The issues that individuals who live all around our churches are dealing with can be heavy and people don't always have the support systems they need to cope or find meaning amid the struggle. Rather than worrying about going to or trying to save an aging institution that seems irrelevant to these concerns, people look elsewhere for belonging, meaning, and ways to cope with the pressures of life.

As United Methodists, we have a message of liberating love—to see people free from cycles of fear, anger, and hatred. The unconditional love of God flowing through our lives offers a solution to the deep ills of our world that people so desperately need. "The spirit of the Lord is upon me to proclaim release to the captives." The life and teachings of Jesus Christ offer freedom from isolation and the endless quest for material gain.

Franciscan priest and author Richard Rohr asks the question, what happens when you climb the ladder of success and get to the top only to find that the ladder is on the wrong wall? This is the gift that the good news of Jesus Christ offers people—to find the right wall, what counts, what matters, and what can transform pain, hatred, and fear. That gift is love—God's profound, unconditional love. That is what we have to offer. But if people are not coming into our buildings to receive it, that message must travel outside the walls of the church. Luckily for us United Methodists, taking the message of God's love outside the walls of the church is inherent in our Wesleyan DNA. So let's jump back in time to John Wesley's day, eighteenth-century England, and look at how the church addressed (or didn't address) the major concerns of society and how John Wesley responded by taking a message to the fields.

The History

A Disconnect between Church and Society

It's always a bit disconcerting to read a history book and have the realization that what happened then is pretty similar to what is happening now. Mark Twain said it best: "History doesn't repeat itself, but it sure does rhyme." This sentiment bears true when we compare today (particularly in the US) to eighteenth-century England. Renowned Methodist historian Richard Heitzenrater wrote a history of early Methodists in which he situated their rise in a particular context (one not too unlike our own): "As we look back on the early eighteenth century . . . what stands out is the contrast between the extremes—poverty and wealth, Jacobites and Republicans, rationalism and enthusiasm, immorality and virtue."[5] Today's church is seen in a similar fashion to the Church of England in Wesley's time. Most people of the eighteenth century were seen as morally lethargic and believed the "church" was lacking an ability to engage them in a way that mattered to them, in a way that connected with them, or in a way that encouraged them to be missionally minded or concerned beyond themselves.

Today, social, political, and theological extremes prevent the formation of community, vulnerability, and joint mission, and instead replace these ideals with narcissism, othering, isolation, and anxiety. Our extremes might be: billionaires and middle/working-class; woke and un-woke; immigrant and citizen; educated and uneducated; Republican and Democrat; progressive and evangelical. In 2022, the wealth gap in the United States was still increasing, with the top 10% of households owning over two-thirds of the country's wealth, and the top 1% owning 27% of the country's wealth. Meanwhile, the bottom 50% of Americans owned 6% of the country's wealth. The average wealth of the top 10% of households is over $7.5 million dollars, while the average wealth of the bottom 50% is $46,000.[6] We can easily get lost in the statistics, but the point is that the stark divide between the wealthiest person and the middle-class worker average person is quite staggering.

Heitzenrater points out that this same dichotomously aligned society also existed two hundred years ago. And while these stark contrasts divide us into seemingly two unmovable ideologies, it also breeds space for creativity, if we have the energy and brain-width to be open to the power of the Spirit! It's in this liminal space where John Wesley developed his Practical Quad. He was able to be an agent of the state, an ordained clergyperson, an incredibly well-educated Oxford don, all while finding new ways of bridging the gap with the dissenter, the unchurched, the uneducated, and the poor. In doing so, he was missionally innovative, constantly responsive, and adaptive to new needs as they emerged.

A Disconnect between Church and Movement

Religion or being religious in John Wesley's day carried with it an air of suspicion no matter your theological leaning. One of the best ways to understand how religious people were perceived is to look at political cartoons of the day. Comparing two satirical engravings by William

Hogarth, a well-known engraver and satirist of the eighteenth century, can help us decipher the distance between the established church and the Methodists:

The first engraving is "Credulity, Superstition, and Fanaticism: A Medley." There are two versions of this engraving. The first was never published and was titled "Enthusiasm Delineated" and has a few more

Methodist overtones than the final engraving, published one year later. The overall setting of both engravings is the same: the interior of a preaching house, complete with an upper and lower pulpit and a crowd of Methodist listeners. The preacher in the upper pulpit is holding a devil in one hand and either a witch or a Raphaelean depiction of God in the other. The pattern under the preacher's robe is of a harlequin (referencing an entertainment aspect) and the words on the pulpit (where his sermon might be) say, "I speak as a fool." The lower pulpit has a cross-eyed preacher (allegedly George Whitefield, known to have strabismus, and the paper on its podium quotes one of his sermons). The congregants are in various stages of ecstasy, some appearing angry, others overwhelmed (to the point of birthing rabbits) or fainting. Others engage in what seem to be overtly sexual or lewd acts.

Sprinkled throughout the engraving are references to Methodism. On the right is what we might call a "religious thermometer," which measures the emotional states of one's brain when exposed to Methodism—from lukewarm in the middle to either love heat, lust, and ecstasy at the top or downward to sorrow, agony, suicide. This religious thermometer sits atop "Wesley's Sermons" as if the message of his sermons is properly measured in this way. In the earlier engraving, the brain that holds the thermometer is directly named as "A Methodist Brain."

This engraving (either edition of it) is often contrasted with "The Sleeping Congregation," which was aptly titled as it depicted the interior of an Anglican church, with a congregation entirely asleep as the preacher sits down and reads from Scripture, using a magnifying glass to see better. It is quite the contrast to "Credulity, Superstition, and Fanaticism" and it was intended to be so. In the hallway of the Wesleys' home in Epworth, between John and Charles's parents' bedroom and theirs hang these two engravings, showing the stark contrast between the two movements. This was the first time I ever saw original prints of these engravings, and it reaffirmed the reason why I began to study Methodist history. There was something that those Methodists were saying that caught people's attention, whether positive or negative.

These satirical depictions of Methodists are surely a response to the radical message Methodists were proclaiming. Historian Richard Heitzenrater contextualizes the eighteenth century as a needed breath after an intense century of religious revolution and religious extremism. The turmoil in the British monarchy meant that the Church of England was characterized by religious persecution between Catholic and Protestant factions. As the monarchy swayed between Catholic and Protestant supporters, various reforming sects formed in response to these tensions. Heitzenrater claims that after these extremes were settled via the Act of Toleration (1689), the eighteenth century became quite religiously (he suggests even morally) complacent:

> The careful restraint, the willingness to compromise, and the desire for balance in all things resulted in a sense of harmony, quiescence, and equilibrium that might very well have caused the lethargy, stagnation, and comfortable slackness that marks much of the English society [of John Wesley's day].[7]

Those who sought to challenge the seemingly quiet norm or "attempt to find a better way were branded as enthusiasts."[8] Thus, Methodists, seeking to reform the Church of England through a renewed sense of outward mission especially with the poor and through faith as enacted love, became one of those people seen to be stirring things up, and therefore labeled as "enthusiasts."

Wesley's Fix: A New Message in a New Place

While John Wesley had a radical message, he didn't yet have a place to preach it. He was not new to the idea of religious societies. His father had organized these types of societies, and they were allowed under the Act of Toleration; however, they were occasionally viewed as potential sowers of dissent. These religious societies were in the background of that group that Charles Wesley and his classmates formed at Oxford, the one derisively labeled as "the Holy Club" that we discussed in the previous chapter.

After Oxford, John and Charles traveled to Georgia to convert the English citizens there and Indigenous nations. This endeavor is mostly considered a failure, as John ran away to avoid an arrest warrant because he publicly denied the governor's niece, Sophey Hopkey, communion. (The typical story is that he denied her communion because of a broken heart, but he actually denied her communion because she married an enslaver and thus, by marriage, broke the rules of the religious society. There's always more to the story!)[9] After the failed mission to Georgia, John was left wandering and wondering where his message of God's love for all would go next. In the early winter of 1739, it just so happened that his friend-sometimes-enemy, George Whitefield, was preaching in Bristol. George had been in Bristol for about one month preaching to growing crowds, but was getting tired of the scenery (and the crowds) and longed to go back to the American colonies for another grand preaching tour. However, he didn't want to leave Bristol unattended since the Methodist movement there was growing. After four other people told George "no," John said "yes."

The city of Bristol was ripe for missional innovation. A city in transition, much of the industrial development that would later become the Industrial Revolution was just beginning there at that time. It was a sea-port town overrun with people seeking industrial jobs and potential wealth. And it was surrounded by coal mines, which provided the (literal) energy to feed this growing industry. It was incredibly filthy and known as one of the dirtiest places in all of England. But, these disparities, this population, and this city became the epicenter for Methodist innovation. It is here that John preaches outdoors for the first time (1739); it is here that the first Methodist building in the world is built (1739); it is here that bands and class meetings are developed (1740); it is here that Wesley builds a school that mixes clergy in training with children of the poor (1748); it is from here that Francis Asbury boards a ship to the Americas to begin to organize Methodism across the Atlantic (1771); and it is here that John assigns himself the power of ordination and blesses the separation of Methodists in America (1784). It is in Bristol where Methodism was birthed, adjusted, thrived, and set loose.[10]

The Quad Begins: Field Preaching

When John was asked to come to Bristol, he probably pictured himself preaching from a pulpit to the industrial elite of Bristol. But that's not what happened. George Whitefield sought to preach at established and respected pulpits, but was too impatient to wait for permission from Bishop Joseph Butler (it was customary to receive the permission of the bishop prior to preaching in their diocese). While he was awaiting Bishop Butler's permission, Whitefield was invited to speak to two religious societies that met in rented accommodations (not in churches). Therefore, preaching to these societies did not require the permission of the bishop, and Whitefield was eager to get to work. There were, at that time, about six religious societies established in Bristol and all of them sought to do some sort of service within their community, such as establishing schools. So while the message and audience of Methodism might have been new, some of the practices weren't.

According to G. M. Best,

> On 17 February Whitefield preached again at Newgate Prison and then opted to go to preach outside the city in Kingswood to some of the colliers who worked in the hundreds of small mines that provided the coal for Bristol and its growing industries.[11]

There was not a parish within five miles of the colliers' village, and the colliers (coal miners) "lived like squatters in squalid, hastily-erected homes, [and] were renowned for their heavy drinking and lawlessness."[12] Thus, it was assumed that no one would pay any attention to Whitefield preaching there . . . even if he was preaching outdoors. Preaching outdoors wasn't "illegal," but it also was one of those acts considered suspect and too reminiscent of the seventeenth-century "enthusiasts." According to George Whitefield's journal, around two hundred people listened to Whitefield's message that while society might shun them as poor and unworthy, God loved them. Whitefield was "deeply moved to see white lines appearing on their blackened faces as they wept at such news."[13] His message clearly met a profound need. In Bristol, what challenged the institutional church was not only the unconventional outdoor location of Methodist preaching, but also—and perhaps more significantly—the marginalized audience and the radical inclusivity of the message.

After preaching in the colliers' fields, Whitefield began receiving and accepting invitations to preach inside of parishes (even though he had still not yet received permission from Bishop Butler) and he balanced those with preaching to societies in preaching houses. Eventually, word got around to the bishop that Whitefield was preaching inside (and probably outside) parishes, and the bishop threatened excommunication. Whitefield cancelled all parish invitations in response and instead maintained his preaching commitments to societies and to the outdoors![14]

Desiring to head back to the American colonies but not wanting to let the steam in Bristol settle, Whitefield wrote to John Wesley (again, John was his fifth choice), "There is a glorious door opened among the colliers. You must come and water what God has enabled me to plant."[15]

Whitefield, smartly, played to John Wesley's organizational skills and ego, claiming that only someone of John's stature and experience could take over. Upon receiving the letter, John consulted his brother Charles, whose own poor experience with field preaching the previous autumn led him to discourage John from the same. However, John wrote to another friend, John Clayton, stating,

> I look upon all the world as my parish. . . . In whatever part of it I am, I judge it meet, right, and my bounden duty to declare unto all that are willing to hear the glad tidings of salvation. This is the work which I know God has called me to.[16]

That's a lot of history for a few pages so let's review the scene: John is in London organizing a religious society, but is still feeling called to do something more—he just doesn't quite know what yet. George Whitefield was preaching to allegedly tens of thousands of people per week in Bristol, many of whom were poor or outcast. John agrees to come see what's going on in Bristol, but doesn't know the whole story.

The day after arriving in Bristol, John heard Whitefield preach at Bowling Green in the open air to approximately six to seven thousand people, followed by a midday gathering at Hanham Mount, and finally at Rose Green to approximately thirty thousand people. Later that evening, John wrote in his journal,

Field Preaching

> I could scare reconcile myself at first to this strange way of preaching in the fields, of which he set me an example on Sunday; having been all my life (till very lately) so tenacious of every point relating to decency and order, that I should have thought the saving of souls almost a sin, if it had not been done in a church.[17]

The next day, John tries preaching in the fields for the first time, preaching in a brickmaking yard, aptly known as the Brickfields. He stated that in this act, he "submitted to be more vile and proclaimed in the highways the glad tidings of salvation, speaking from a little eminence in a ground adjoining to the city, to about three thousand people."[18]

According to many who were there, his sermon was not necessarily well received; however, he kept on, eventually filling preaching rooms to the literal breaking point (during one sermon, the cumulative weight of those gathered broke the wooden planks of the floor, leading to hundreds of bodies crashing down to the earth!).

Why the History Matters

We share this history in order to ground us in the fact that by preaching in a field for the first time, John not only rejected the rules of the institutional church but also its typical audience and message. He expanded the circle of those deemed worthy of God's love to include the outcast—coal miners, the poor, the illiterate. He delivered the same message to them that he would give to established or elite congregants inside parish walls. For John, neither the setting nor the audience altered the fundamental truth of God's universal love for all humanity.

Taking the message of God's love outside the walls of the church was risky. John became an immediate target of ridicule (about which his brother had warned him). But John knew that there were people around him who did not feel comfortable inside the parish walls. And the laboring class rarely, if ever, had the Sabbath off to attend their local parish. So taking the message from the parish and into the fields was not only transgressive but also liberative. It allowed people who had never heard that they were worthy of anything to hear that they were worthy of all.

Today's Call to Field Preaching

The church today faces a critical moment of surrender. We must release our grip on failing traditions and acknowledge that our conventional approach is no longer effective. This surrender requires abandoning the illusion that people will simply return to our sanctuaries to hear our message. But surrender also means yielding to something greater—like a swimmer submitting to powerful currents rather than fighting against them. When Wesley chose to become "more vile" by preaching outdoors, he embraced what was culturally unthinkable because he recognized a greater purpose. His field preaching wasn't a trendy innovation but a deliberate strategy to meet people where they lived—all to deliver the transformative message of God's unconditional and liberating love.

Clinging to "church" as merely a building threatens our very relevance today. We carry transformative truth in fragile vessels—a message the world desperately needs for healing, renewal, and liberation of the brokenhearted and oppressed. We must embrace what once seemed beneath us: uncomfortable spaces, unknown methods, uncharted territories. Our motivation isn't trendiness or FOMO (Fear of Missing Out), but rather avoiding FOBO—the Fear of Becoming Obsolete. We surrender to God's liberating Spirit moving through our moment in history. The imperative is clear: if people won't enter our doors, we must go to them—into fields, marketplaces, workplaces, and public squares. But what does this Spirit-led outreach look like in our digital age?

Many campus preachers deliver messages of damnation and doom to passing students, yet standing in fields, city squares, or grocery store parking lots rarely proves effective for communicating liberating love in ways that genuinely connect with today's people. Field preaching in the twenty-first century is as varied in form as it was in the eighteenth century and can manifest in many ways. In his seminal work, *Jesus and the Disinherited*, Howard Thurman said that the call of Jesus to love compels us to meet people where they are and treat them as though they are where they ought to be. This encapsulates the golden rule—do unto others as you would have them do to you—which does not depend upon the condition, but the force of unconditional love.

Just as love compels us to meet people where they are in the ordinary spaces of life, the message of love must travel into the fields where people work and play and into the third spaces that shape their daily experiences. In our present culture, we easily feel very uncomfortable taking religious messages into public or workspaces, afraid to feel manipulative, coercive, or forcing our faith upon others. Field preaching today doesn't have to look like shouting a message of doom at people who walk by, but instead like setting up a little well where people might find refreshing drink and otherwise barren landscape.

Over the last several years, I (Chris) have changed my own entertainment patterns away from music in the car and television at home to podcasts and YouTube interviews and videos and shorts throughout the day and on long trips. Today, through content available in asynchronous media, I can literally listen to anything about anything. I can either enrich my life or clutter up my brain with garbage. I have gone down some deep rabbit holes learning about vintage guitars and the stories behind some of my favorite music heroes. I have listened to stories and learned about the creative processes of some of my favorite comedians. The content available to me is richer than it has ever been and more abundant. How do I choose, and how do the messages find me? In a day where we are bombarded with misinformation, negativity, and rage, I long for messages that could be positive, lift me up, or be a breath of fresh air.

Field Preaching—Not the Destination

The dirty little secret of Methodist history is that while John Wesley traveled over an estimated 250,000 miles, preaching over 40,000 times, most of which were not from church pulpits, he actually despised field preaching. For him it was a cross to bear for the purpose of meeting people where they were to set them free, a means to an end.

But what was that end? Why did Wesley endure bad weather, threats of violence, mud and muck?

Community

In order to live the Christian life people need to be in direct relationship with one another, living out their faith as a shared experience. Field preaching is not the destination, but a crucial first step in Methodism's method for the purpose of meeting people where they are and getting them into a communal experience of the Christian life in action.

Preaching in the Market Square

In the world of marketing theory there is a common model used to describe how to engage prospective consumers and turn them into repeat customers called the "marketing flywheel." This model rotates as a circle moving people from "Attract" to "Engage" to "Delight," and back through the whole cycle again. While field preaching is not intended to be a consumerist or commercial endeavor, it does compete with other media and messages for people's time and attention, often in the same platforms and spaces as commercial messages. Anyone who uses digital technology as a platform of modern-day field preaching has to break through the noise to connect people with a message that they deem to be worth their time and attention. Such messages rely on the nature of their content or delivery to attract and engage people with something that is different from everything else that people can find online. In a season of anxiety and misinformation, a hopeful message that runs counter to negativity can make all the difference, especially when sharing the news that a loving God can liberate us from a cycle of fearmongering, hatred, and violence. Just as Wesley preached in the market square where other merchants sold their wares, modern forms of field preaching may use the same platforms, digital and physical, where ideas that run counter to our values are made accessible. To understand how digital spaces can be leveraged as modern fields where we can proclaim a message of God's love that people need to hear, I will explore examples from a few different popular platforms.

YouTube

The second-most popular search engine online, YouTube hosts a seemingly endless repository of user-generated and commercial content covering virtually every topic, genre, and purpose that a person could ever want to see. During the COVID-19 pandemic many churches reluctantly explored YouTube as the virtual home of their online worship services and subsequently many preachers have added their sermons, either live-streamed or pre-recorded, to the sprawling collection of content that would-be pursuers could find. However, most local church content doesn't play the algorithm game well enough to garner any more than 100 views, while other, more viral videos can quickly attract hundreds of thousands to millions of views. One of the reasons that sermons don't break past their own localized viewer base to appeal to a broader audience is because they lack elements that might help them stand out in an otherwise crowded marketplace.

Rev. Nathan Webb, who goes by "Nerd Pastor Nate," planted an online-only church called Checkpoint Church—"a church for all people, especially nerds, geeks and gamers." Nate records a short message every week on YouTube that connects the gospel message to online gaming and popular culture references that would speak to a particular audience that otherwise wouldn't wander into a church building. The benefit of this form of field preaching is that it is accessible to anyone anytime and anywhere who has access to YouTube. The message can be accessed from around the world whenever someone has time to listen. The gospel travels out of the building to meet people where they are.

Most importantly, this preaching happens in a field that doesn't get a lot of preachers bringing a message of God's unconditional love amid the world of gaming and anime.

Shorts

The fastest growing form of online communication is short-form videos, popular across different social media platforms. Videos lasting just seconds or up to three minutes long can capture a user's attention and deliver any message it wants. When used as field preaching, a short can be an excerpt of a longer sermon, podcast, or video that makes an inspiring point. As is for other forms of field preaching, a short existing as a singular message unto itself has limited impact. But if a short attracts people to further explore an account, similar content, or other media that can deliver additional messages, it can serve as a means for larger impact. I have begun to follow many different speakers, influencers, and preachers because of a compelling short that I saw on my social media feed. Shorts have a brief moment to make an impression, which puts the emphasis on the content itself. When using shorts to get across a message of God's liberating love, focus on one point, or one brief message that will catch someone's attention; offer an inspiring thought; and be sure to connect it to a social media account, website, or other online source where people can go deeper in exploring your message.

Live Broadcasts

Another online form that became popular by necessity among churches during the pandemic is live-streaming or live-broadcasting. While many churches still use different platforms to live-stream their worship services, there are other uses of the live format that are perhaps better suited as a method of field preaching, including prayer, live conversations, and sing-ins.

During the pandemic I began to tune in to the live morning prayer time that pastor/author Rev. Rachel Billups would faithfully host each morning, greeting people as they logged on and naming their specific prayer requests. While she began this practice before the shutdown in 2020, the need for a hopeful word and communal prayer discipline made her daily broadcasts a lifeline for many, compelling her to continue to maintain this practice beyond the pandemic. The livestream platform has given her the opportunity to proclaim a message of hope and faithfulness to thousands of people who otherwise might not have known of her ministry or received inspiration on a given day. Other leaders and ministers have broadcast daily prayer time to interact with viewers in real time in order to create connection and to offer an alternative message to the anxiety, rage, and negativity that is too readily available in social media spaces.

Composer Mark Miller has also used live broadcasting during days in which tragedies, or other difficult moments, have taken place in order to bring people together by offering sing-ins. Live sessions of singing his own original songs along with engaging with live viewers' questions and comments have served as a communal event for people who have come to know Mark through his music and performances around the world. Such use of live streaming has served a field preaching function by bringing an inclusive loving gospel message, connecting with people outside of the church as well as connecting friends, pastors, professors, and students with one another in hopeful community during otherwise challenging moments.

Email Devotionals

Even though email is a saturated information marketplace where people often feel inundated with too many messages in their inbox, individuals and organizations are still using compelling email campaigns to deliver powerful messages and subsequently form communities of people who hold in common the values of love, hope, and liberation. Different preachers, teachers, leaders, and heads of organizations use regular email campaigns effectively connected to other platforms like video, Substack (paid subscription site for online writing), social media, and websites.

While there are many examples of thoughtful leaders who use email campaigns well for the sake of offering inspiration, few have used email as consistently well as Father Richard Rohr, who is the founder of the Center for Action and Contemplation in Albuquerque, New Mexico. For well over a decade the CAC has sent Daily Meditations, which are devotional in nature but are often excerpts from his books, sermons, and lectures that articulate spirituality from the contemplative Christian tradition in a way that resonates with lifelong Christians and non-Christians alike. Drawing from Scripture, ancient mystics, and his own wisdom as a Franciscan priest, Rohr has used these daily emails to grow a large international community of 380,875 individuals receiving the emails each day in 2023 (according to their annual report: https://cac.org/support-cac/annual-report-2023/#:~:text=In). Rohr's Daily Reflections have served the function of field preaching as they met people where they are with a message of God's liberating love and connected them with the greater community of the Center for Action and Contemplation.

Podcasts

While shorts have taken the social media world by storm, there is still a great demand for long-form media, such as podcasts and video interviews. I often hear the assumption offered in church circles that everyone wants to receive information in short bits and therefore messages have to be short. This is true for certain types of messaging. However, at the same time, podcasts, which can last 2+ hours, continue to grow audiences of listeners and viewers. Leveraging a podcast as field preaching uses the same principle that Wesley used: enter the marketplace and offer a different kind of message. A podcast that offers a message of hope, grace, and God's liberating love is in itself preaching in the field.

I recently launched my own video podcast called "Love, the Goal" as a form of modern-day field preaching, intended to explore positive themes to counter the endless negativity that dominates my social media feeds. Each podcast episode, found on YouTube and podcast apps such as Apple, Amazon, and Spotify, is an interview with a different pastor or leader discussing what it means for them to put love into practice as Jesus teaches, which includes love of neighbor, the enemy, the stranger, the sick, and the sinner. Each featured guest has dedicated their life to loving people in difficult and challenging spaces that illumine the beauty of transformation that comes when we are persistent. In an interview with Shane Claiborne, he tells a story about receiving love in a profound way when he went to Iraq with a group of Christians to show solidarity for people living in a war zone. When Shane's convoy hit an IED and he and others were rushed to the hospital, the doctors who cared for them refused payment other than a promise that the group would go home and tell the story of the people they met there. When Shane, surprised, exclaimed, "Wow, there are Christians here!" the doctor reminded him that Christians in Iraq preceded those living in almost any other part of the world. This humbling and transformative experience reminded Shane of God's constant love and movement beyond our comprehension, which compels him to "go and do likewise."

The "Love, the Goal" podcast was created to offer a different type of content in stark contrast to the steady stream of negativity and rage that is too readily available online. The interviews were intended to inspire and model a "more excellent way" of loving others in a hurting world. The learning for me is that field preaching as digital content can be exciting, as it can reach far beyond any geographical region and can meet people where they are in unexpected ways and places. It also taught me that content creation is a grind as you seek to hold attention. In the world of streaming content, you are only as good as your most recent (and highest viewed) post.

Just as the giants of streaming, Netflix, Disney+, Hulu, and Amazon have found, followers and subscribers can be fickle fans, only sticking with a service as long as there is something interesting to binge watch. The moment there doesn't seem to be anything new that is interesting enough to watch, the subscriber may drop the service and find new content elsewhere. This lesson is important to remember once we identify the realm of digital content creation as a form of field preaching today. Just as preaching outside was not the final destination for John Wesley and the Methodists, content creation to proclaim liberating love in digital spaces is only a means to an end. Otherwise, clergy must free themselves from all other responsibilities in order to keep up with the never-ending pace of video production and social media engagement. These are important, but exist for a purpose greater than inspiring or entertaining the viewer (or listener). Field preaching exists for the sake of stirring in people a longing that will lead them to what they desperately need—community.

In-Person Field Preaching Today

Of course, field preaching today doesn't have to take place online but can happen in any unconventional space or location that meets people where they are with a message of God's liberating love. The Fresh Expressions movement, started in the UK and now flourishing in the US within The UMC as well as other denominations, seeks to plant ministries in nontraditional spaces such as tattoo parlors, coffee shops, outside parks, and anywhere else people gather. Engaging in proclamation of the word can come in many forms such as art, drama, spoken word, music, discussion, and interviews.

A form of field preaching near and dear to both of us is an effort called "Beer and Hymns" that was brought to the Arkansas Conference by Ashley's mother, Rev. Rebecca Boggan, and a few of her partners in ministry. While it doesn't sound very Methodist on the surface, the effort sought to have hymn sings in local pubs engaging people in spiritual songs and hopeful secular songs for the sake of making new connections outside of a church building. Today, Beer and Hymns is a 501(c)3 nonprofit organization that hosts pub sings to create spiritual communities in non-traditional spaces while also raising money for charitable organizations. Today this would easily qualify as a Fresh Expression of church, but it has been from its original design a form of field preaching to meet people where they are to bring a message of God's liberating love.

From the Fields to the New Room

Within months of John Wesley preaching outdoors for the first time in Bristol, the group of people who amassed in response to his preaching created a society that needed a space, one that would enable them to gather and serve the vulnerable in that community. They had tried to assemble in other spaces but they outgrew each one. They now needed a new room to gather. After buying a little piece of land in the town, John Wesley built them a "New Room," which remains the first and oldest Methodist building in the world to this day.

Field preaching today can look like a lot of things in a variety of contexts. It can look like "Tattoo Stories," which takes place in a tattoo parlor in Ocala, Florida, planted by Rev. Michael Beck as a fresh expression to help people share the stories of their tattoos and hear about a God that loves them no matter what. It can look like a nerdy sermon video from Checkpoint Church, or a YouTube interview with people practicing love in challenging but beautiful spaces. Field preaching takes place when we leave the pulpit and church building to meet people wherever they may be to share a message of God's liberating love.

But that is not the stopping point. We cannot bring people to Christ and expect them to organically grow in faith or be nurtured as disciples. John realized this in Bristol. He saw that the people who were gathering to hear his words would benefit from some sense of organization. This is where John begins to construct the second part of the Practical Quad: micro-communities. He asked himself a question: how do you keep those who have been convicted by a message of God's love connected to one another and growing in their faith?

The answer for John: "bands."

The answer for us: "micro-communities!"

Notes

1. Letter March 3, 1739, published in *Arminian Magazine* 1797, 18–19.

2. John Wesley, "Entry April 2nd, 1739," in *The Journal of John Wesley*, ed. Nehemiah Curnock, vol. II (London: The Epworth Press, 1911), 172–73.

3. "Report on Disaffiliating United Methodist Churches through 2022: Comparing Similarities and Differences," Lewis Center for Church Leadership, February 28, 2023, https://www.churchleadership.com/leading-ideas/report-on-disaffiliating-united-methodist-churches-through-2022/.

4. Office of the U.S. Surgeon General, "Our Epidemic of Loneliness and Isolation, 2023, https://www.hhs.gov/sites/default/files/surgeon-general-social-connection-advisory.pdf.

5. Richard Heitzenrater, *Mirror and Memory: Reflections on Early Methodism* (Kingswood Books, 1989), 34.

6. "America's top 10% controls 60% of the wealth. The bottom half holds 6%," *USA Today* (October 24, 2024), https://www.usatoday.com/story/money/2024/10/24/americas-richest-10-percent-controls-60-percent-of-wealth/75790850007/#:~:text=The%20report%20found%20wealth%20inequality%20on%20the,of%20wealth%20in%201989%20and%20in%202022.

7. Heitzenrater, *Mirror and Memory*, 35.

8. Heitzenrater, *Mirror and Memory*, 35.

9. Bobby McClain, *Black People in the Methodist Church: Whither Thou Goest?* (Cambridge: Schenkman Publishing Co., 1984).

10. G. M. Best, *The Cradle of Methodism* (Tangent, 2017), 22, 25–26.

11. Best, *The Cradle of Methodism*, 30.

12. Best, *The Cradle of Methodism*, 30.

13. Best, *The Cradle of Methodism*, 30.

14. Best, *The Cradle of Methodism*, 31.

15. Letter March 3, 1739 published in *Arminian Magazine* 1797, 18–19.

16. JWJ, June 11, 1739.

17. JWJ, March 3, 1739.

18. JWJ, April 2, 1739.

MICRO-COMMUNITIES

"How is it with your soul?"

"Directly opposite to this is the gospel of Christ. Solitary religion is not to be found there. "Holy solitaries" is a phrase no more consistent with the gospel than holy adulterers. The gospel of Christ knows of no religion but social; no holiness but social holiness. "Faith working by love" is the length and breadth and depth and height of Christian perfection."[1] —John Wesley, foreword to Hymns and Sacred Poems

> **Micro-communities**—groups of persons gathered to hold one another accountable in and to God's love, allowing the grace of God to be present within, flowing through, and acting out from each individual.

The second, and perhaps most essential element of the Practical Quad is the formation of micro-communities. If field preaching were the ultimate goal of Christian evangelism, then the fruitfulness of the endeavor would rely on the impact of single messages. However, the genius of Wesley's method was that meeting people where they were outside was not the end goal. Field preaching was a means of inviting people into community where they could form relationships and grow in their faith through social holiness. Sharing the life of faith with other people seeking to follow Jesus, watching over one another in love, is perhaps the singular defining aspect of the Methodist movement that would spread around the world. Methodist bands, class meetings, and societies gave people places of belonging, mutual accountability, and friendships as they grew in their faith.

Today, the specifics of what is discussed and how the groups function and adapt may be different in each context, but the same principle remains true: participating in micro-communities is central to the method of methodism and is where the heart of what is unique to our movement is found. Micro-communities are also where mutual care is practiced, and members find belonging, support, and peer mentoring in the life of faith. While there has been significant emphasis placed on the role of small groups within the church in recent years, the original form of Methodist micro-communities that prioritizes soul tending over curricula or Bible studies has not been given enough attention. Given the current climate in which loneliness and isolation impact the lives of so many, it is imperative that churches meet people where they are with a message of God's liberating love for the sake of connecting them in micro-communities where they can grow in faith in the context of meaningful relationships. But where do we start?

The Problem Today:

If a majority of people in our communities are no longer coming into our churches to encounter a message of hope, the word can travel to them through a form of field preaching. But then what? Are those engaged in ministry to become tethered to the never-ending hamster wheel of content creation hoping to continually inspire people? Even though spirituality has become a genre of self-help literature, the message of God's unconditional love requires more than just the acts of proclamation and receiving a message. To live as Jesus followers, loving God and our neighbors, we cannot do it simply by listening to a podcast and we cannot do it alone. The love of God requires relationships.

Growing up in rural Pennsylvania, I remember asking my dad about signs that were posted on the back roads near our house: Weight Limit 10 Tons. He explained that while 10 tons seemed like a lot of weight, commercial dump trucks and tanker trucks often exceeded that weight and were too heavy for tar and chip, which is a softer, cheaper asphalt used on rural roads. Similarly to road weight limits, bridges have their own limit that they are designed to support. If a truck carrying a load heavier than

10 tons were to travel on one of these rural roads, or a small local bridge, it would likely get stuck, or worse, the road or bridge would collapse.

Relationships between people are like bridges and roads. They can only carry a load commensurate with the strength of their design and construction. The more they are fortified and strengthened over time, the greater the load they can handle. When too much strain is put on a relationship through conflict, miscommunication, or differences of position before we have built up trust or mutual commitment to the relationship, the relationship can crumble or buckle. The more we invest in healthy relationships, making deposits in trust, appreciation, and friendship, the greater load the relationship can handle.

The primary challenge today is that society is becoming more transactional than relational. As technology advances, our ability to conduct business and carry out daily life functions becomes more efficient, but it also becomes less personal and relational than it once was. It is less likely today that people know their neighbors, doctor, mail delivery person, or local store owner than we would have decades ago. Make no mistake; I love modern technological conveniences. I'm thrilled that I can do my banking, check my own medical chart, pay my bills, and even send money to family living far away through a smart phone app. Yet there is an unspoken opportunity cost. The more we can do through technology, the less we are forming communal and meaningful relationships, only increasing the sense of isolation and loneliness described by Surgeon General Murthy.

When it comes to the practice of faith and spirituality, it is becoming easier and more popular to utilize technology to find inspiration, and engage in spiritual practices such as yoga, meditation, and prayer. With the rise of those who claim no formal religious affiliation, the pursuit of spirituality through individual means has resulted in greater emphasis on the individual and less on community. Even within the church, steady decline in congregational size has placed an emphasis on numbers and metrics that record the number of people present at worship services, classes, and events, rather than on the stories or result of the experience.

When John Wesley published his collection, *Hymns and Sacred Poems*, he included several texts that were traditionally used within the Anglican Church, but engaged a mystical understanding of faith that longed for solitude and an experience of the divine away from the presence of other people. Sensing the need to correct what he perceived to be faulty theology, although still not excluding the hymns from the collection, Wesley wrote in the foreword to the hymnal that individual Christianity is incompatible with Jesus's teachings in the Gospels.

> Directly opposite to this is the gospel of Christ. Solitary religion is not to be found there. "Holy solitaries" is a phrase no more consistent with the gospel than holy adulterers. The gospel of Christ knows of no religion but social; no holiness but social holiness. "Faith working by love" is the length and breadth and depth and height of Christian perfection.[2]

Wesley was clear. To be a Christian, a follower of Jesus, relationships are necessary. Even a step further, the good news of Jesus can only be lived out in the context of community. When we practice our faith by loving God and our neighbor, we have captured the fullness of Jesus's message. We cannot practice love, as Jesus teaches it, without being in contact with our enemy, the foreigner, the stranger, the sick, the prisoner, and the poor. To be a disciple, community is not optional, but is at the center of our life in faith. But, somewhere along the way, the central component of class meetings and bands was phased out within Methodism in America. As we reclaim the centrality of micro-communities to our method of faith formation, it is important to understand their history.

The History

Two Frenemies: John Wesley and George Whitefield

There are many places and spaces where John Wesley, in our opinion, outdid George Whitefield. Wesley's expansion includes not only his Arminian theology—believing that all persons and not just "the elect" were worthy of salvation—and Wesley's anti-slavery position (vs. Whitefield's use of enslaved labor to build schools in the colonies) but also,

Wesley's ability to build community. Whitefield was potentially the better preacher—or at least he attracted bigger crowds. Tens of thousands of people allegedly came to hear Whitefield's sermons, and he was arguably the first "celebrity" Methodist preacher—someone with a great speaking voice, but also someone without a genuine connection to community or desire to build community.

John Wesley was just the opposite. Despite being an itinerant preacher, John cared deeply about the communities in which he preached. Arguably no town witnessed this more than Bristol. It's here that Wesley's ministry is forever changed when he finally allows himself to "submit" to the will of God, doing something he never ever thought he would do, where he allows himself to be "more vile" and go against his own (and society's) standards of decorum. When he preaches in those fields the first time, he is marking this moment and this place as different. But, again, unlike Whitefield, John doesn't simply preach and leave. He stuck around—and for quite a bit. John realized the impact that his (and Whitefield's) preaching was having on those in Bristol—especially the colliers and their families. And he realized that in order to keep people engaged with their faith and to help their faith grow, he had to do more than just preach.

One of the key characteristics of early Methodism was an adaptive, innovative response to problems as they arose. John quickly created a new means or method of addressing any number of issues and would sometimes implement them before he really had thought through all of the potential outcomes (good or bad). This adaptive, innovative, immediate response to problems is one of the crucial characteristics that undergirds John's method that we've lost as The United Methodist Church. Today, any change we want to make, from the local congregation, to the district, annual conference, jurisdiction, or general church has to go through committee after committee and is subjected to substitution, amendment, being tabled, or flat-out ignored. Furthermore, in order to change things at the general church level (which is where they sometimes will have the widest effect or the widest potential replication), the change has to wait until the next General Conference, which normally happens every four years. And if we're being entirely honest with how we as United Methodists do things, any truly innovative idea will only be voted upon after a study committee has analyzed it for at least one quadrennium. As Methodists, we've completely lost our ability to respond in a quick, innovative manner. Instead, we've begun to be content with complacency, order, and things getting lost in committees. Slow, committee-reliant, institutionally driven mission and polity. This is not Wesleyan missiology or ecclesiology. His method of doing church was innovative. His method of disciple nurturing was responsive. We need to take a lesson from our past and be adaptive; the Practical Quad is a tool for just that.

The Quad Continues: Micro-communities

Few of John's ideas were brand new, or even of his own mind. His genius came in listening to others. When it comes to Wesleyan innovation, it is not necessarily about reinventing the wheel; it's finding new purposes for the spokes that exist. For new purposes, John often looked to what was working in other faiths, communities, and places.

Once again, we begin to see this innovation in Bristol. Within weeks of preaching in the fields in 1739, John realized that those who had gathered to hear field preaching needed a method to sustain their faith. Their souls had been awakened via a message of God's love and their worthiness within God's eyes, but how do you keep them awake if they simply go back to the lives they were leading? This is where John stepped in and borrowed a concept he had learned from the German Moravians—bands.

Bands were one of three types of micro-communities that John would bring to the people called Methodist. Bands (and their even smaller subgroup "penitent bands") were the most vulnerable level. Composed of four to six people who had something in common with one another (and divided by gender), bands were essentially spiritual accountability groups. They were a space that allowed Methodists to openly discuss their fears, their joys, their temptations. It was a micro-community where someone asked, "How is it with your soul?" It was a place to discuss where God was showing up in one's life, and where one felt they had turned away from God. Bands were a quick fix and model of nurturing discipleship, and when balanced with the societies in London and in Bristol, bands provided a more intimate spiritual connection to one another that ultimately kept people coming back to the society after having been spiritually awakened by field preaching.

But where were the bands to gather? During one of John's sermons at the Back Lane Society in Bristol, so many people had gathered to hear him preach that they began to strain the integrity of the wooden floor. Within a few minutes, a loud, distressing sound was heard as the floorboards began falling apart. Hundreds of people plummeted to the ground below (but still listened to the sermon as John kept preaching). The problem: one of the preferred meeting and preaching houses in Bristol had collapsed. Without hesitation, John began constructing a new preaching room, and cleverly called it The New Room. Opened in June 1739, this building was used to accommodate the increasing crowds who gathered to hear Methodists' message, but more importantly it provided a space for bands to meet. It quickly became more than just a preaching house, however. The New Room would serve as a library, a medical dispensary, and a market, and included apartments upstairs for itinerant preachers. This was the first Methodist building in the world—and it speaks volumes to the importance of Bristol that it was in this town that John built the first official preaching house of Methodism.

The Class Meeting

The next problem was how to pay for construction of The New Room. John was famously not wealthy, although he did receive a sizable income as an Oxford fellow. But he gave away as much as he earned, keeping only what he needed for the bare minimum of life. His audience was not necessarily wealthy either, as he was preaching predominately to colliers and those of lower classes. So how do you pay off debt when no one seems to have cash flow? By 1742, John had an answer—a new level of micro-community, the class, with a very specific mandate: tithing.

The class, like the band and society, were not John's idea. It was actually the idea of Captain Foy, a member of Methodism in Bristol. He suggested gathering about a dozen or so persons together and tasking a class leader with collecting one penny per week per person.[3] Rather quickly, however, the class became about more than just tithing. It transformed from a fundraising platform to another micro-community, and became a place where John could check his follower's theology.

Enter again George Whitefield. John Wesley and George Whitefield preached different messages, with John's theology based in Jacobus Arminius, and Whitefield's theology based in John Calvin. The easiest way to differentiate their foundations is to simply say that John believed that Christ died for all persons and that humans have agency in choosing to acknowledge God's work in their lives; Whitefield believed that Christ died for only a select few persons and those persons had no agency in whether or not God had chosen them. As Methodism grew, both John and Whitefield maintained the label "Methodist," and those who followed them, despite their different theologies, all identified as "Methodist." There were even more types of Methodists springing up by the late 1740s who didn't follow John or Whitefield. To further complicate things, there were Methodists who were outright breaking the rules of the institutional church—and not necessarily rules that John was okay with breaking. Some Methodists were preaching in unregistered preaching houses. Others served communion outside official parish walls. By the early 1740s, John began to differentiate and clearly define the Methodists for whom he was responsible.

When reading John's 1740s tracts (and some sermons), in his first few paragraphs, he'll often say something along the lines of "by Methodist, I mean. . . ." And this is where he differentiates Wesleyan Methodists from other Methodists.

The class became a micro-community that functioned as a checkpoint in the long journey of salvation people. If it had been talking about being "elect" or had been seen taking communion outside of a parish, then the class would hold them accountable by rescinding their ticket. It was a place where theologies were checked and where people were reminded of what John desired for his Methodists.

The class meeting also became the micro-community that was most easily replicated. When Irish Methodists began to migrate to the colonies, they established class meetings in the colonies as early as 1765 (six years before Francis Asbury would arrive to begin organizing Methodism in the colonies and nineteen years before The Methodist Episcopal Church would be created). There are two origin stories of the Methodist class in the colonies.

The first origin story involved Methodists in and around the Maryland area. Irish Methodists arrived sometime between 1760 and 1766, settling in Franklin County, Maryland. Led by Robert Strawbridge, these Irish Methodists recognized that in their rural area there was not a nearby parish that they could regularly attend. Having been a Methodist preacher in Ireland, Strawbridge began a class meeting in order to provide his community with spiritual direction and accountability. Out from this class meeting emerged other class meetings (this is a hint at the leadership activation piece that we'll examine in chapter 4). From there they spread not only in numbers but across Philadelphia and Virginia. Today, a shrine marks the location of his home and of the Old Stone Church, one of the earliest Methodist chapels built in America.

The second origin story also begins with Irish Methodists coming to the colonies, settling in what is now Lower Manhattan around 1762. A woman named Barbara Heck believed that by 1765, her community of Irish Methodists had become too complacent in their faith. One evening, Barbara walked into the parlor of her home and found her cousin (and former Methodist preacher) Philip Embury doing the unthinkable—he was playing cards! Barbara, almost unable to contain herself, gathered the cards up in her apron and threw them into the nearby fire. She then looked at Philip and said, "You will start a Methodist class meeting." And on October 12, 1765, he did.

The class meeting began in their home, but quickly had enough people attending to need a larger space. They rented out a sail rigging loft around the corner, but that held the crowd for only a few months. Eventually they purchased a small piece of land on John St. and built Wesley's

Chapel. The original location of Wesley's Chapel is now John St. UMC in Lower Manhattan and is a Heritage Landmark of The UMC.

Connecting Micro-communities:

And finally, John's genius was not in developing these communities (again, none were his idea alone), but in how he connected these micro-communities to one another. The best way to think about the different relationships and the different types of faith development that happened in each level is to use some words from our modern ecclesiology.

Bands were the smallest and most intimate group. They were where you could truly open up and reveal your pains, confess your temptations, and celebrate your accomplishments. I think of this as a Sunday brunch bunch. Who are the four people that you feel comfortable spilling your soul to over a pitcher of mimosas or a pot of coffee?

The class was the place where you went to hear others exhort (or testify about their faiths), to sing, to pay your dues, and to be held in check that you were living your faith out in an intentional way. It was kind of like Sunday school. It was a consistent place to gather weekly where you exposed your faith to different opinions and hopefully it deepened as you listened to others. And those other persons made sure that you showed up and were living a life of love.

The society was the largest of the micro-communities. It was sometimes forty to sixty people. It was where you went to hear a Methodist preacher, to sing hymns, to be convicted of sin, to be reminded that you are whole, and to revive your faith. Think of this as your local congregation. You are connected and recognize one another because you gather together, but you aren't as intimately familiar with everyone there. You are most likely part of the same society because of where you live and probably no other reason.

Why This History Matters

For forming micro-communities, John was heavily critiqued by other ordained Anglicans. They did not like that John encouraged people to engage with one another outside the church walls of the Anglican church (gasp, I know!). He was accused of creating schism, of "gathering churches out of churches." To this, he responded,

> If you mean only "gathering people out of buildings called churches," it is. But if you mean dividing Christians from Christians, and so destroying Christian fellowship, it is not. . . . We [Methodists] introduce Christian fellowship where it was utterly destroyed. And the fruits of it have been peace, joy, love, and zeal for every good word and work.[4]

This quote speaks to one of the perennial problems of "doing church" today. Within our busy schedules, church time is often (if at all) relegated to Sunday morning, preferably for one hour, prior to noon (because football!). One of my favorite things to remind United Methodists of today is that the original Wesleyan Methodists did not meet on Sunday morning. Methodism grew and expanded because it provided a space for spiritual growth outside and beyond Sunday morning. It was focused on Sunday afternoon through Saturday evening and encouraged people to attend to the state of their soul throughout the week through micro-communities. And it did this in a place/space that was often convenient for people—in their homes, in a pub, or in a coffee shop. You didn't have to go to the church building to receive spiritual care. John knew that micro-communities needed to exist throughout the week and in a variety of spaces to truly sustain faith. We need this sense of creative community building today, perhaps more than ever.

Today's Micro-Communities

Surgeon General Vivek Murthy wrote a follow-up document to his 2023 report, "Our Epidemic of Loneliness and Isolation," called, "My Parting Prescription for America." In it he describes how his father, who grew up in rural India, never felt more poor than when he moved to the US and experienced the loss of community. Even though most of the people in his village growing up experienced poverty and tragedy, he explained that the close-knit intergenerational community banded together to provide meaning, support, and purpose for its members. Without that community in a new country, he felt the loneliness and isolation of being cut off from relationships. Murthy goes on to underscore how important community and relationships are for our thriving physically, mentally, and spiritually. Without them, our overall health and well-being suffers. So what do we do about it?

At the beginning of my pastoral ministry, I (Chris) visited South Korea with my bishop and a group of pastors and laity. The role of cell groups within the many Methodist churches we visited there was immediately apparent. In order to be a part of the church, in many of the ones we visited that had thousands of members, a person had to belong to a smaller cell group. This micro-community gave a sense of belonging, spiritual nourishment, and mutual care among the members. To be an active member of the larger church community, you first had to be active in a smaller, more intimate community, where people could form deep relationships. During the trip our group was reminded that this model was not new to the church in South Korea, but had been a central part of the method of Methodism from the beginnings of the movement under John and Charles Wesley in England.

The fact, however, is that the Wesleyan model of bands, class meetings, and societies was dismantled and replaced in the American church in the 1800s as Sunday school became the growing trend within the institutional church. Most of us on the trip belonged to churches that had few, if any, active small groups. Most of us longed for, or planned to start, small groups, but we had only wished that we could develop a model as well organized and functional as what we had encountered in The Korean Methodist Church.

In my own personal experience as a pastor, I have tried many times and ways to plant new small groups only to experience the same issues over and over again:

- The problem of synchronicity
- Issues over curriculum or content (what to teach/how to lead)
- The problem of inclusion/exclusion (closed/open groups)

The Problem of Synchronicity

One of the biggest and most frequent issues around trying to start anything new within the church quickly becomes a problem of scheduling. People's lives are busy and over programmed much more than they were when Sunday School classes and class meetings used to thrive. But more than the fact that people are busy, our lives are less synchronized on the whole than they once were. Our weekly schedules are no longer tethered together by common television broadcast schedules, workdays, or store closures. With streaming entertainment, work from home, and 24-hour shopping options, most people are on their own schedule which differs from even their own peers, friends, and family.

Any effort to get a group of people together, especially those who work full-time and have children at home, stalls out upon the realization that there are not common meeting times available to the majority of potential members. Some people can do mornings, others early evenings, while still others can only do once the kids have gone to bed. Meeting after church is bad for people with kids in sports; Sunday evenings don't work for the parents of kids who have to finish homework and get ready for a new school week. Did I mention that Saturdays are out for people who play golf, like to travel, have family members in sports, work weekends, are in grad school, dance, need to do yard work, or have any sort of social life? As silly as it all sounds, the struggle to assemble people at a common time is real, and if the value of the program does not rise above all of the other competing priorities, people will never commit to it. This leads us to the issue of trying to compete for value against every other option people have at their disposal. "So, what do you do in a small group anyway, just read the Bible?"

Issues over Curriculum or Content

A challenge that has proven even more critical to the survival of a given small-group than finding common meeting time is answering the question, "What do we do in the small group?" Different churches have different approaches and even small group programs that answer this question in a variety of ways. Some small groups serve as support communities for people in similar affinity groups, such as a parents' group, or a retirement group, a grief support group, or one for the parents of differently abled children. Another common approach is the book-study or curriculum approach. The group agrees upon a particular book or resource to read together and study. Of course, there is always the more traditional Bible study group that vary greatly in approach from reading a biblical text line by line and having members of the group reflect on what they are reading, to using another study resource that explains in depth the background of a biblical text.

While each of these models is valuable and has its own place in the life of the church, they don't fill the same role that the early bands and class meetings filled, which was to share the experience of living out faith for the purpose of "growing in grace" and "watching over one another in love." In my own personal experience, most curriculum, topical, book, and even Bible studies focus on what people think or believe, which easily turns into a place of debate and eventually division. Like a road with a light weight limit, groups that are not built on strong relationships first quickly erode and crumble when people disagree on theology, politics, or opinions.

While long-time church goers may enjoy debating a theological position, more often than not people who need community the most—people who are going through a divorce; parents who have a child with a serious health condition; someone struggling with addiction, depression, or any sort of personal crisis—are much less likely to stick around for a group where people bicker about their opinions on a given topic. Absent the deep relationships necessary to navigate differences and difficulties, a group will quickly be reduced to the same church people who attend everything else at the church at the expense of those who are seeking and in need of real community. People who feel unmoored in life don't need another place to debate opinions, they need the very thing that is increasingly more difficult to form: authentic, meaningful, and healthy relationships.

The Problem of Inclusion/Exclusion

If a group is able to find a common time to meet and once they have decided what the content of their small group will be, the next obstacle is this nagging sense that every offering in the church should be open to all people all the time. Therefore, a church might advertise that there will be a Tuesday night small group meeting each week at 7 p.m. As the weeks go on some people might try the group and decide it isn't for them. Others might only come once a month. Over time the makeup of the group might change so much on a weekly basis that there is a different group dynamic every meeting, making it difficult, if not impossible, for people to form real, trusting relationships with one another.

The alternative to the aforementioned "open group" model, which can literally be a different group every time it meets, is the "closed group." A closed group is not generally publicized as being open to anyone to join at any time for the sake of forming deep relationships and maintaining a high level of commitment to participation and confidentiality within the group. I have personally had the experience of trying to form what are called "closed groups" in one church that I served, only to be faced with the criticism that they would become cliques and would directly work against the goal of inclusion and radical welcome of all people into the life of the church. Even though limiting new members once a group has been formed or requiring a vetting process to the admission of new members can lead to a stronger sense of trust, being known, and knowing one another, there is often the perception that anything closed or not open to everyone is bad within the church. This is why we prefer the term micro-community.

A Place for Life-Changing Relationships

Micro-communities are exactly what they sound like: smaller communities within larger ones. When Wesley set up the class meetings, they were micro-communities of the larger Methodist societies. The smaller communities, classes, were divided up by physical proximity—a group of up to twelve people who all lived near one another. This community within the community deepened belonging both among the class but also within the society, as people who had deeper and closer relationships were overall more committed to the cause of Methodism and more likely to become a leader. In the same way, the cell-groups within several of the Korean Methodist churches I visited were either arbitrarily formed based on when people joined the church, or by where people lived, and became an individual's support system within the much larger congregation. After seeing how the Korean cell-groups functioned within very large churches I realized that was similar to how residents of New York City (or residents of any major city) function.

All New Yorkers have a unified identity as a New Yorker, even if they live in different boroughs, or root for different sports teams. But, important to any New Yorker's identity is their neighborhood. You aren't just a New Yorker, you're also from one of the five boroughs and from a particular neighborhood in the borough. It is in the neighborhood where you shop, know your neighbors, and develop daily routines. Being a part of the greater community of people within the city unites. The close-knit and shared relationships of a neighborhood don't threaten the experience of being a part of the city, but only strengthen and enrich it. Of course, if you never leave your neighborhood for any reason, don't visit other neighborhoods, or learn about any other part of the city, that doesn't make you a particularly good resident of the city. In the same way, being a part of a micro-community can be life changing and deepen one's experience of a church community. However, if a group is unhealthy and inward focused only, it does not truly serve the real purpose of micro-community within the Methodist method: embodying and sharing love toward God and one another.

Watch over One Another in Love

The well-worn pathway in the traditional church model of church leadership is to place people on committees. There is an implied understanding that serving on committees is a logical way for individuals to make new relationships and grow in their commitment to the church.

However, in my experience, committee service, particularly as churches shrink and struggle to function as they once did with more people and more resources, has a tendency to burn out good people, especially younger new people. The issue is that while people want to serve, what they need and long for more than anything else is to feel that they are loved and find a sense of belonging. When people argue or bicker over church budgets, how to care for aging facilities, or personnel matters, individual hurts can come out in all kinds of ways. The committee can get caught up in debates that aren't about what they are really about. The debate over whether or not to add cameras in the sanctuary is often about people's own sense of personal grief, loss, or fear of the unknown instead of the topic at hand.

Newer people coming into a church need relationships more than anything else, even when they want to serve. One of my predecessors in ministry was known to say "people will let you get away with a lot as long as they know you love them." Having served the same church for twenty-five years, Rev. Dr. Charles Sayre knew that when people felt known, loved, and cared for they would be much more able to navigate conflict and difference in the church. He also understood that people who had significant healthy relationships within the church made for the strongest and most reliable leaders. Too often people are placed into demanding roles without feeling loved or known. When that is the case they are often easily displaced when they experience discomfort or stress.

One of the reasons that micro-community is so necessary in the church today is that being in a community of faith is inherently stressful. Differences over culture, politics, theology, and approach to ministry can easily divide people and make for conflict. Micro-communities provide the space for people to get to know others at a deeper level and to grow in their own ability to experience and share love. The stronger our primary relationships are, and the more grounded in the experience of sharing God's love, the easier it will be for the community to navigate the pressures that inherently arise. Also, the more that people are able to grow in their faith in the context of loving relationships, the more spirit-filled the church becomes. Wesley used the language "watch over one another in love" as a function of the Methodist micro-communities, which perfectly captures the role of modern expressions of micro-communities.

The Grace Group: A New-Old Model for Today

GRACE GROUP GUIDE

Purpose: To grow in grace and watch over one another in love

--- Center ---

Offer prayer or a moment of silence to center the groups as you

1. Soul Tending
How is your faith journey going?

2. God Sightings
Where are you experiencing God moving in your life?

3. Growing In Grace
What is one challenge you are working through that you need to offer over to God?

--- Close ---

Close in prayer for one another.

Knowing that micro-community is important and forming micro-communities are two different things. Attempting to bring the right mix of people together, choosing the model or content of the group, and determining when the members can meet can be challenging. When I encountered the stories about the formation of the early Methodist bands and class meetings while in England, I realized that the beauty of Wesley's model was in its simplicity. There are several different lists of the questions and class meetings. While in England, I realized that the beauty of Wesley's model was in its simplicity. There are several different lists of the questions used by early Methodists in their various micro-communities recorded in letters and other historic documents. Common to all of them are simple inquiries into the state of a person's faith life, their spiritual practices, and the things that they struggle with. The simplicity of a few questions is what gave the class meeting model its power for people to share their lives with others. That same simplicity also helped the model to spread all across England, to Ireland, and to the American colonies. Eventually, the same simple micro-community model spread to South Korea where I encountered the cell groups that were Wesley's legacy generations later.

Grace Groups

After a deep dive into the class meeting methodology of the early Methodists, I determined that I, as well as many Methodist leaders, have been overcomplicating things. Instead of using trendy curricula, book studies, and other small group resources, the simplest way might yield the greatest fruit. As a result, I developed a simple guide for groups to use that asked three basic questions along three simple movements:

- Soul Tending: How is your faith journey going?
- God Sightings: Where are you experiencing God move in your life?
- Growing in Grace: What is one challenge you are working through that you need to offer over to God?

I called this simple model of micro-community a Grace Group, with the primary purpose of the group being to "grow in grace and watch over one another in love," which is firmly rooted in Wesley's vision of the early Methodist classes. I have since planted a number of Grace Groups within and outside of my congregation by forming groups of six to eight people and asking them to begin and end their time with some sort of prayer or centering and have each person share their answer to the three questions.

To be honest, it sounded too simple and perhaps a bit too personal. However, after piloting several groups I began to see incredible results.

One of the groups I piloted was developed specifically for my doctor of ministry project, seeking to test the Practical Quad that is proposed in this book with younger adults. The group was made up of seven people under the age of thirty-two, each of whom was nominally involved in the church and all of whom felt disconnected from peers in the church. Even upon meeting for the first time, each person shared a response for every question in the Grace Group Guide with vulnerability about their hopes, faith journey, and struggles. After six weeks, I asked the participants to rate their ability to experience God's presence and love, as well as their ability to love as Jesus teaches us to love in challenging ways, such as loving our neighbor, enemy, stranger, and the marginalized. Pre- and post-project self-assessment surveys were used prior to the start of our first meeting and after two months of meeting in order to measure change in these abilities.

A majority of the members, six of the eight, showed significant positive movement in their net growth scores. One person showed no net change, and one declined in rated ability. The post-project survey also asked a number of open questions that reported exceedingly positive feedback about the experience, particularly regarding the Grace Group meetings. Members shared how meaningful it was to form relationships with people their own age who believed in God and were trying to apply their faith in everyday life. Other answers spoke to the power of hearing one another share of how God was moving in their lives. While loneliness and isolation pervade in our society, journeying in faith by reflecting on and answering three simple questions within a micro-community consistently over time might just help people strengthen the relationships they need with God and others to help bear the heavy loads people often carry.

Along with the DMIN pilot group, I have used this guide in a variety of spaces as well as shared it with others who have adapted it and used it in a restaurant, at home, in a coffee shop, on Zoom, in a college seminar, and of course, in a church. While micro-communities have looked differently over time depending on where they were formed and who was leading them, the point remained the same. Faith in Jesus Christ cannot truly be lived out alone. Following Jesus requires love and love requires relationships. Tending one another's spirit lives is the core method of Methodism. However exactly we choose to do it, it is a tremendous gift that changed the world and has shaped the church around the world. To reclaim the method of Methodism we must reclaim Wesleyan micro-communities that are not book studies, courses, or even Bible studies, but rather an experience of people seeking to grow in grace and watch over one another in love.

Grace Groups Can Happen Anywhere

Recently Ashley spoke at a university and had the opportunity to conduct breakout sessions with students. She organized the students into smaller groups and asked them to use the Grace Group Guide for about an hour to guide them in conversation. The students loved it. Keep in mind these were groups that were formed in the moment without much work in building a group dynamic, although they were peers and mostly already knew one another. The form of the group questions was directive and open enough to allow for the students to share openly and to deeply listen to one another. For participants who were in the primary demographic of the population that has been struggling with isolation and loneliness, the Grace Group met a need.

I have found the same to be true in other settings, including a workshop for the Fresh Expressions movement, in which we asked people who were in a newly formed breakout group to use the guide for their conversation. In each setting people began from a place of consent and a desire to share in this way with others. I have been repeatedly surprised as to how deep people go quickly and because there is a structure with questions to guide the conversation, people listen without interrupting or debating. Participating in a small group experience that doesn't quickly turn into a debate or conversation about politics, theological positions, or the "right way" to think is refreshing. Instead, it is giving people a place to share their lives with one another in the context of care-full listening and a common desire to grow in their experience of God's presence.

The truth is that with a basic structure that is simple enough to be adapted, translated, and contextualized, you can form groups in homes, cafes, restaurants, outside, and in any culture or setting. The goal isn't to debate opinions, but to share life in faith. In an age of isolation and disconnection, Wesley's model of how people of faith can "watch over one another in love" can be a balm for people's spirits.

The Heart of the Practical Quad

If one element among the four is central both to the method of early Methodism and to what can transform the church today, it is microcommunities where people can find belonging, engage in mutual care, and share their experience of God work in their life. You don't have to wait to organize a program or system. Try the Grace Group model within your Bible study group, choir, church council, or other teams. Done within the context of mutual love and with a good moderator, it can transform a group dynamic and reshape how people look for God's presence in their lives and even in the church.

Among the Methodists in Bristol and beyond, the growth of the class meeting marked not just the growth of Methodism as a spiritual practice, but the expanding of social engagement and action, as members of the societies and classes were expected to care for the marginalized among them and to respond to the hurts and needs around them. This would quickly result in the founding of the Kingswood School, a school for the children of poor miners, as well as the distribution of medical supplies, food, and other resources that were a direct response of Jesus's teaching to care for "the least of these." No one among the Methodists was exempt from showing love to their neighbor in tangible ways. So, today, as we form and multiply microcommunities as the heart of our own faith formation work, we have to let go of any notion that mission is for a committee and move every person to the next element of the Practical Quad: social engagement.

Feel free to use this Grace Group Guide (below) or download it online at www.abingdonpress.com/calling-on-fire-extras and begin to walk alongside others today to grow your collective experience of God's love in your life.

Living Out Discipleship in a
Grace Group

A *Grace Group* is a small group of people who commit to meet regularly, and share their discipleship journey with one another.

Purpose of Covenant Groups:
To grow in grace and watch over one another in love

How it Works
Meet regularly in person or online to share in Soul Tending, God Sightings, and Growing in Grace moments, as well as pray for and encourage one another

A *Disciple* is a follower of Jesus who puts faith into action, is growing in grace and being perfected in love

Three General Rules of Christian Discipleship
1. Do no harm
2. Do good
3. Practice the Means of Grace

The *Means of Grace* are practices that help us experience, confirm, and grow in the grace of God

Devotional Practices		Practices of Solidarity	
Individual	Communal	Individual	• Seek justice
• Read scripture	• Worship	• Do good works	• Work toward
• Prayer	• Communion	• Visit the sick	ending
• Meditating	• Small Groups	• Visit those in	oppression &
• Fasting	• Bible study	prison	discrimination
• Healthy living		• Feed the hungry	• Care for the
• Sharing faith		• Give generously	needs of the
		Communal	poor

Notes

1. John Wesley and Charles Wesley, *Hymns and Sacred Poems* (Strahan, 1739), viii, accessed May 24, 2024, https://divinity.duke.edu/sites/default/files/documents/04_Hymns_and_Sacred_Poems_(1739).pdf.

2. John Wesley and Charles Wesley, *Hymns and Sacred Poems.*

3. G. M. Best, *Cradle of Methodism*, 139.

4. John Wesley, *Plain Account of the Methodists*, Works of Wesley, volume 9, 258–59.

SOCIAL ENGAGEMENT

"Love has to spin outward"

"Above all remembering that God is love, [the Christian] is conformed to the same likeness. [They are] full of love to his neighbor: of universal love, not confined to one sect or party, not constrained to those who agree with [them] in opinions, or in outward modes of worship, or to those who are allied to him by blood or recommended by nearness of place. Nor [do they] love those only who love [them], or are endeared to [them] by intimacy or acquaintance. But [their] love resembles that of [the God] whose mercy is over all his works. It soars above all these scanty bounds, embracing neighbors and strangers, friends and enemies; yes, not only to the good and gentle but also to the evil and unthankful." —A Plain Account of Genuine Christianity, *1753*[1]

"I reminded the United Society that many of our brethren and sisters had not needful food; many were destitute of convenient clothing; many were out of business, and that without their own fault; and many were sick and ready to perish. . . . I desired all whose hearts were as my heart: 1. To bring what clothes each could spare, to be distributed among those that wanted most; 2. To give weekly a penny, or what they could afford, for the relief of the poor and sick." —John Wesley, *JWJ, May 7, 1740*

> **Social Engagement** is going out into the world, hand in hand, in Christ's love to learn from, work alongside, and transform the world for the better.

The third component of the Practical Quad is social engagement, or more explicitly, engaging the hurts and needs of the world while seeking justice and peace for all people. While micro-communities serve as the centerpiece of the method of Methodism, practicing the love of neighbor is essential to the faith that is lived out in community. Although "mission" is often relegated to committees or a few mission-minded people within churches, for Wesley and the early Methodists, engaging the hurts and needs of the community and greater society was not optional. Living as a scriptural Christian meant following the commands of Jesus, including the call to "do unto the least of these" and loving one's neighbor in tangible ways (Matthew 25).

The key to the Practical Quad is that it is not a menu with different items to choose from, rather it is a method that renews itself through the flow of energy between and among the different components. As we love our neighbor, engaging in relationships across boundaries for the sake of sharing God's love, our own experience of God's love is renewed. Just as feeding the hungry, caring for the needs of the poor, and working to end unjust practices such as slavery and inadequate food provisions were acts central to the life of Methodist societies, social engagement and the work of social justice play an indispensable role in spiritual formation today. Once we have created micro-communities where people can find belonging through mutually loving relationships, how can we then shift our focus to share God's love across boundaries of socio-economics, race, age, and culture for the sake of participating in God's mission? To begin, we look at the distinctly Wesleyan emphasis on the means of grace that place us in deep solidarity with our neighbor.

The Problem Today

It can be deeply liberating to find your people: the people who accept you, the people with whom you can connect and grow. A few times in my life, I (Chris) felt like I had my people around me. But, in each season it was only a matter of time until something changed the social dynamic of a group of friends, colleagues, or a small group at church. Someone would move; we would all graduate; the organization would change; or people's roles would shift or go away. The feeling of acceptance and comfort with others can be an elusive feeling that we end up chasing much of our lives.

When we find acceptance, we don't want it to change, but, inadvertently, life changes and we can fall out of comfort or belonging.

On a Wesleyan history tour at Oxford University, I was in conversation with our guide, Methodist historian Paul Chilcote, about the Practical Quad proposed in this book. When I began to explain the microcommunity component, Paul interjected: "You have to shift the focus to move outward. Love *has* to spin out, otherwise your group will lose inertia and collapse inward." Chilcote was referring to an understanding that he proposes in his book *Recapturing the Wesleys' Vision: An Introduction to the Faith of John and Charles Wesley*. In it he states that John Wesley's theology was conjunctive, both/and, bringing together polar notions. In particular, it is Wesley's understanding of the means of grace that our experience of love must move inward toward God (piety) and then flow outward to our neighbor (mercy/solidarity) like a figure eight, renewing its own energy through motion. If we focus only on ourselves and God, the energy declines and dissipates. But if we move from our relationship with God to sharing it with others, both experiences renew the flow of love and keep us connected to the spirit.

I have found this to be quite true in my own life and ministry. When we focus only on ourselves, even if it is on our relationship with God, it is only a matter of time until disciplines are abandoned and momentum is lost. But when we move out of our comfort zones, crossing boundaries for the sake of sharing love, we can find renewal, perspective, and a deeper experience of God's grace. Many times, over the years, I have heard people who have returned from a mission trip say, "Somehow we feel that we received more than we were able to give." That's the point of Wesley's understanding of the means of grace. When we do as Jesus taught—to feed the hungry, visit the sick, and welcome the stranger—both parties encounter the love of our creator God anew. The experience becomes a means, or conduit, through which we experience God's grace. This is why Wesley knew that if Methodists were to live as true, scriptural Christians, they must spin love outward to care for the hurts and needs of the world.

While Wesley had been "spinning out" (pun potentially intended) with love since his Oxford days, the incorporation of social engagement into the method of Methodism began to be further woven into the developing system in Bristol. It is here that the various components begin to unfold and be intentionally connected into a method: field preaching, micro-communities, activism, and leader activation. This chapter will focus on activism as a key component of the method.

The History

Early Social Engagement in Oxford

We discussed the etymology of "Methodist" in earlier chapters. However, it's worth a brief summation because many United Methodists have forgotten or intentionally strayed away from the why we were/are called Methodist.

Going to set the scene, once again: John Wesley, Charles Wesley, George Whitefield, William Morgan, and a couple of others were at Oxford around 1730, give or take a year. Charles had begun a religious society among them in order to increase their attentiveness to their own faith and to hold one another accountable to their own faith. (Note: these persons were not members of the society at the same time.) Across the years, however, their faith began to be acted out in the world, among and outside the walls of Oxford as acts of love. This meant that accountability to their faith was no longer simply based upon rising early, daily devotion, daily prayer, and daily journaling (what some refer to as **acts of piety** or **personal holiness**). It increasingly involved, and increasingly centered upon, outward acts of love (**acts of mercy** or **social holiness**). According to historian Richard Heitzenrater, "[Early Methodists] expended more energy in acts of social concerns throughout the city than in acts of corporate devotion within the walls of the university."

It is at Oxford where John begins to connect personal holiness and social holiness on his own faith journey. Personal holiness is that one-on-one connection that we have with God; where we know that God loves us, became human for us, and died for us to all be forgiven. As Methodists, integral to our one-on-one connection to God is an interlocked and immediate connection to community, to others, neighbors and outcast. For John, you *cannot* love God *without* loving neighbor. This is what Paul Chilcote refers to when he describes the "spinning outward." If we only focus on ourselves, on our relationship with God, and on our faith and salvation, then we will collapse inward. For John, focusing your relationship with God outward, bringing others to God, ensuring that they have the ability and capacity for spiritual formation and basic happiness was integral to one's personal faith. True faith could not exist in a solitary situation; true faith had to be in community with others. And that community had to be an *active* community, also looking outward through intentional acts of love. If the community only focused on itself, on its communal faith, it, too, would collapse inward. So the community, as a body, must bring God's love out into the world.

One of the earliest examples of this social engagement was begun by William Morgan, who was invited to join this "society at Oxford" by Charles Wesley. Morgan is given credit for suggesting that the "Holy Club" begin visiting persons imprisoned around Oxford. While others might have perceived the Holy Club to be a bit odd, it wasn't until "the small company of friends began to take their program of piety and Christian concern to the prisoners and poor people of Oxford in August of 1730" that their "notoriety increased." And they didn't stop there. The Holy Club contributed to a local charity school, the Grey-Coat School, and provided a teacher for twenty poor children who attended. John and the Oxford Methodists known for giving money to those imprisoned, usually to pay their debts or bail (this included Thomas Blair discussed in chapter 1) and for handing out food to those who were hungry.

Oxford Methodists socially engaged with the most outcast through intentional acts of love to the point that "this combination of serious stewardship and personal concern for the plight of the poor became a hallmark of the Methodist movement."[2]

Social Engagement in Bristol

After preaching in the fields in 1739, John Wesley's preaching calendar quickly filled. When preaching to colliers and to the Bristol established classes, John began to notice stark dichotomies in standards of living. The "Poor Laws," begun in 1601, classified poverty as "having housing (a tenement) worth £10 or less per year."[3] The laws "increasingly tried to put everyone to work who could work, attempted to train children, and endeavored to relieve the aged and infirm."[4] Those who lived above the poverty line were required to pay a "poor tax" to provide relief to those below the poverty line, even though many paying the tax were just above the poverty line. According to Heitzenrater, "The system inflicted especially undue hardships on single women, widows with dependent children, and married laborers in rural areas," and these categories just happen to be the same categories that flocked to Methodism.[5] By 1760, at the heart of Methodist growth, most of the English population would have been classified as "the working poor." If you were to survey the class lists around this time, it appears that the Methodists were "slightly poorer" than the average English person. Heitzenrater argues that "65 percent of Methodists belonged to occupational groups whose income averaged less than £20 per year, while 25 percent were in groups that averaged over £30."[6]

John chose to categorize poverty not along a clear demarcation of income, but in relative terms. For him, "The poor were those who lacked the necessities of life."[7] Whether it be food, clothing, or housing, most who lacked necessities were victims of a rapidly changing economy, one that was for centuries centered on a pastoral system and was quickly shifting to an urban, industrial system. In his analysis of John's relationship with the poor, Heitzenrater argues that "Wesley declassified the concept of poverty, identified the breadth of the problem, and universalized the responsibility for dealing with it."[8] He measured poverty or wealth not in terms of pounds per year, but in terms of contentment—was a person's life "sufficient, decent, or adequate"? Even those who were considered relatively impoverished, John argued, could still contribute in some way to those around them and could always find someone who was worse off than they were. As he encountered poverty more and more, he came to understand wealth as having anything more than the necessities of life.

By the 1760s, as John encountered the economic diversity around England, he began to critique the idea that the poor were lazy and indolent. Instead, he argued that "the problems of hunger and unemployment were caused by poor government policy, economic management, and societal choices."[9] Instead of Band-Aid fixes, John sought to address real, spoken needs through systemic change where all parties (even those classified as impoverished) participated. Heitzenrater argues that John categorized persons by needs and then provided a variety of ways to meet those needs:

> First, to relieve the *helpless* (the impotent poor), he took nourishing food to the hungry, collected decent clothes for the threadbare, and furnished adequate housing for widows and orphans. Second, to assist those who were *unfortunate* (the able poor), he boosted their employment by sending the weavers yarn for their looms and establishing a loan program to distribute seed money to struggling merchants or manufacturers. Third, for the *children*, Wesley established schools to train the minds, bodies, and spirits of young boys and girls. Fourth, for the literate but *uneducated* adults, Wesley established a prolific publishing program that provided important literature for his people—much of which was produced inexpensively—to be given away to those who could not afford to purchase it. Fifth, to assist the sick and infirm, Wesley hired apothecaries and doctors to staff free medical clinics in his preaching houses in London, Bristol, and Newcastle. Behind these programs lay a desire to encourage industry, thrift, learning, health, and godliness.[10]

Education

As more persons were listening to him preach, more persons began to express interest in becoming Methodist preachers. Perhaps due to his mother's emphasis on equitable education (she famously taught her daughters to read before she taught them to sew), John understood that a primary means to address social inequity was via education. In 1747, he constructed a school in Bristol that taught Collier's children basic academics, providing them with the skills to move up the economic ladder later in life. Seeking to connect different social and economic layers of the community, John placed the colliers' children in the classroom with those adults who studied theology, seeking to be Methodist preachers. And so those who sought to be future Methodist preachers were studying alongside those whom they would be preaching to. Genius.

Malleable Space

A second example of Wesley's social engagement was the building of The New Room itself. As mentioned in the previous chapter, The New Room was the first Methodist preaching house in the world and was financially supported through members' contributions via the class meeting. Every person, no matter how poor, was expected to contribute—the idea being that when we give what we can, it will all be compiled to assist the greater good. The New Room was quite unique; when a person pictures a preaching house, I'm sure they picture pews and a pulpit. The original structure of The New Room did not have pews! Can you imagine walking into a modern sanctuary and not seeing pews? Instead, Wesley used mobile wooden benches that could either be lined up for listening to preaching or pushed aside for other events. You see, in today's lingo we might call The New Room a community center or a multipurpose building, for at the heart of Methodist preaching was the call to act out faith as love. How could Methodists preach this message and not use their physical spaces for more than preaching? The New Room became a library, a medical dispensary, a market, apartments, and a gathering space. It was responsive to new missional and social needs and its malleable space allowed it to be so. Imagine what our physical buildings could host if we were able to push aside the pews and the pulpit and open people up to access the Spirit and Love of God in that room.

In researching United Methodist spaces and places that are doing this type of radical and rooted ministry, I (Ashley) stumbled upon Rev. Michael Gienger, (co)pastor of Central UMC in Galveston, Texas. Michael has been serving alongside this community since 2014 and has transformed it from a dying congregation into a thriving space that does ministry differently (and in a very Wesleyan rooted way). You step into Central UMC and instead of pews, there are couches. The second floor of the building hosts a medical clinic, where medical students from the local medical school provide free, accessible, nonjudgmental healthcare. Most of those who attend the church are unhoused, rehabilitated, parolees, or undocumented. There are no questions here, just love. Those who attended Central UMC feel like they have a safe place to return to, a community that cares for them and their well-being above all else, and a space that is truly judgment free.

These types of spaces and communities that utilize their physical spaces in ways to address the multiple malleable needs of a community while doing radical forms of social engagement are exactly what John envisioned. It is exactly what the ministries that the New Room was created for and exactly the heart of social engagement that Wesley sought for those early Methodists. How do we radically love those around us, those cast out? How do we embody radical hospitality that has people wondering "why are those Methodists welcoming and affirming of anyone?"

Equitable Access to Healthcare

John didn't just build multifunctional spaces though; he also sought to change the hierarchy of need. The institutional church then (and now) tends to focus on spiritual needs first: save the soul then save the body or hook them before you help them. This is absolutely horrifying missiology and is not Wesleyan. John prioritized addressing physical necessities first, as his experience had demonstrated that individuals cannot focus on spiritual concerns when experiencing physical discomfort. Given the lack of medical access and equity in the eighteenth century, John began to dabble in medical sciences, reading anything he could find and chatting to apothecaries and professionals. He wrote the first *Primitive Physick* in 1747. Today we might call it a manual of home remedies, and it was meant to be just that. He intended to provide proven ways for addressing basic ailments in any English home using the herbs or ingredients that most households had access to. Some of the remedies suggested have withstood the test of time: drinking water with honey to address a cold, exercising daily, and ensuring adequate sleep. However, others, in today's medical practice, are a bit humorous. Are you experiencing balding? Try rubbing an onion on the top of your head (or wherever the baldness is occurring) repeatedly for one week. Does your stomach ache? Lay down on the floor and place a warm puppy on your tummy. Seriously though, the theological contribution of the *Primitive Physick* was that it reconnected body and soul as both in need of dire care, attention, and sustenance. And it called upon the faithful to attend to both body and soul.

Why the History Matters

Wesley truly believed that systemic poverty could be remedied if everyone contributed what they could and were willing to socially engage with one another through loving acts. Heitzenrater takes this argument as far as claiming that "at the heart of Wesleyan theology and the 'method' of the Methodist mission" was "love and empathy."[11] While we are arguing there are a number of practical components to the Practical Quad perhaps Heitzenrater has a point: the motivating factor behind the Practical Quad is an active, engaged love of neighbor.

When Jesus says, "You will always have the poor with you" in Matthew 26:11, he is speaking of the perennial nature of human need as a result of injustice and inequality. Far from justifying its causes or encouraging resignation in the face of social injustice, Jesus challenges his followers to lift up the power of what his presence can do among those who hurt or are marginalized. Too often today Christians divide along the lines of evangelism and social justice. Many faithful people believe that the goal of mission and service is ultimately evangelism and conversion. For people who believe that spiritual salvation is the primary goal of evangelism and ministry, any focus on social justice, the plight of the marginalized, and efforts to change systems that perpetuate injustice are a distraction from the main point. Some might even argue that social justice as a focal point of the church is not of God, as it allegedly neglects salvation and spiritual holiness.

While some see social justice as a distraction away from evangelism as the primary goal of religion, conversely, others perceive evangelism as a vestige of colonialism, exclusive, judgmental, and even culturally invasive. Throughout history, efforts to missionize, proselytize, and convert entire nations and peoples have entailed horrific acts of violence, abuse, cultural appropriation, and even genocide. In response against such historic acts and out of a desire to undo centuries of colonialism, imperialism, and racial and cultural supremacy, there are many within the church who prioritize the work of social justice and social engagement as the primary work of faith with a resistance to efforts to evangelize or teach faith systems to people outside of Christianity.

While evangelism and social justice are sometimes adopted with an either/or approach, both elements are central to the message of Jesus and work together to create the spinning energy of God's renewing love. Being led to love the God who created us and who gives all things life spins us inward toward that loving embrace, while sharing the love, grace, and compassion that we gain from God with others spins love outward beyond our own wants, needs, and problems. People who wander into church buildings as a part of recovery communities often come to understand this concept more fully than some of the members of those same churches, particularly those who put the focus on their own spiritual needs over the needs of others.

The 12-step recovery community holds at its core that addiction is the result of many forms of "self." When we are driven by self-centered pursuits, self-centered fear, and a self-focused existence, we can lose connection with God, leading to the need to self-medicate and ultimately self-destruct. That is why "service" is an important element of the triad—unity, recovery, and service—the primary elements of the recovery fellowship. Holding service positions is not just something good to do; it is crucial to recovery. Making coffee, setting up chairs, sponsoring others, and speaking at meetings gets a person out of their own self-centered world to help others. In helping others, one finds a reprieve from toxic self-centeredness one day at a time. Wisdom from the church basement has something to reteach those who dwell in the sanctuary.

The need to serve others was central to John Wesley's theology and the methodology of the early Methodists. In order to reclaim not just our identity as Methodists, but the power that brought personal and social renewal around the globe, it is imperative to reclaim the role of social engagement as something that is everyone's responsibility. Too often "mission" is seen as charity that is given through money, volunteerism, or collections by a committee or small group of the church on behalf of the greater congregation. Wesley understood that Jesus's call to love in uncomfortable spaces and across boundaries was a personal responsibility for all people, not to be delegated or relegated to a few representatives.

Today it is a common story for congregations to experience tension between the worshiping community and a few members who run a food pantry, thrift store, or other social service ministry over the use of space and the financial resources needed to run the ministry. A common criticism that is levied by worship-goers is that the people served by the social ministry don't ever become members or contribute to the church budget. The counterclaim is that social ministry is the real work of people who worship the God who calls us to "do unto the least of these." And yet, the question about financial stability is a valid one: how will a social service ministry be able to thrive in the future if the worshiping congregation that makes it possible dies out over a short period of time?

The practical questions are important to consider, but the question of mission is even more important. What is the mission of the church: to make worshipers or to feed the hungry? The answer is a resounding YES! The mission is to make disciples of Jesus Christ for the transformation of the world—a both/and mission requires a both/and methodology. The key to fulfilling the church's mission isn't ultimately in the simple function of worship or feeding, but it is about God's love in motion through relationships. Just like the micro-community component focuses on embodying the love of God through relationships, engaging the hurts and needs of the world around us is also all about relationships. Rather than focusing on the transaction of food distribution, clothing donations, financial aid, or even services like tutoring, or immigration legal services, Jesus followers engage people and love them across difference, trusting that God meets them there.

Loving Our Neighbors Across Boundaries

Regardless of what the need is, whenever people within the church consider addressing the physical needs of others, they often use the term "mission." Whether it's taking a trip to another country to build homes, sending supplies after a national disaster, or collecting food, the label "mission" indicates that it helps others beyond the church. The natural question to ask then is, "Whose mission?" Is mission the work of those who have resources having pity on those without, and, therefore, sharing their resources by giving money, collecting food, or building something?

Mission theologian David Scott asserts that when we work to address the effects and causes of injustice, we don't embark on our own mission but rather join in the mission of what God is already doing in the world. Therefore, we aren't merely delivering aid or providing help, but we are engaging in mutual relationships in which both parties share God's love, with each having something to give and something to receive. "God's mission calls us not merely to form relationships, but to cross boundaries to form relationships with those who are different from us." When we engage social issues and hurts caused by injustice through the work of "mission," we are intentionally forming relationships with people from different social locations from our own, including socioeconomic, racial, cultural, gender identity, geographic, and privileged status.

Just as the early Methodists addressed a broad variety of social and physical needs, depending on what the specific issues were in each community, the work of our people must focus on the real and tangible needs that affect our neighbors. By focusing on relationships and the flow of God's love spinning outward, we first determine who our neighbors in most immediate need are and what boundaries need to be crossed. It is easy today be overwhelmed by the hurts and needs all around us, let alone those across the nation and world that are highly visible through digital media. However, when Jesus responds in the Gospels to the lawyer who asks him the question, "Who is my neighbor?" by telling the story of the good Samaritan, he focuses on a direct encounter. Loving our neighbor pushes us to pay attention to those in our midst who are different from us. But how can we move beyond our own walls to not only see but know our neighbors?

In order to help churches do just that and bridge the gap between historic churches and the rapidly changing communities in which they are situated, my United Methodist annual conference in Greater New Jersey hosted a Lilly Grant–funded program called "Bridges." Geared toward churches that no longer reflect the surrounding community, the year-long program was designed to guide a team from each church through a process of storytelling and listening in order to learn about the local community. As the church gets to know who their neighbors are and what the needs and opportunities are for ministry, the church is supposed to develop one ministry that addresses a need and builds new relationships within the community.

As a team from my congregation embarked on this work, it became clear that a common need in our local community matched well with a growing passion within our congregation, which is accessibility and support for individuals and families of those on the autism spectrum. Several members of our church's team are part of the neurodivergent community, and, as they engaged the greater community, they began to hear concerns and needs similar to their own. Families expressed a desire to find welcoming community for their children on the spectrum as well as wanting the wider community to learn more about autism so they would be more equipped to embrace and welcome neurodivergent people.

The program that was designed was a full-day neurodiversity conference, with leading experts from medical, psychological, and vocational communities, along with vendors, sponsors, and organizations that offered resourcing on the topic. The pilot event engaged both neighbors as well as church members who were on the margins of the community but felt included and embraced through the event. Two of the members of the Bridges team from my church happen to be in the first Grace Group I piloted. Their service to the congregation and their commitment to engage their neighbors outside of the church are a result of their growing experience of faith and their growing desire to join God's mission beyond the boundaries and borders of the church. The love they have encountered within the Grace Group is beginning to spin outward, and they are sharing it with their closest neighbors in most immediate need.

Social engagement is nothing new to Methodism. Remember: it is the original reason that John and Charles Wesley, along with their friends, were given insulting labels like "Holy Club" and "the Methodists" in the first place. Throughout Methodist history, social engagement, addressing both the immediate needs and the root causes of social ills, has been a hallmark of both the movement and the church. By reclaiming the method of Methodism through the Practical Quad, we are not claiming to do anything new, but rather to connect the components together that help people experience the flow of God's love through their lives, which can hold as much power today as it did some 300 years ago.

To follow the pathway, a message of God's liberating love travels outside of the church to meet people where they are through some form of field preaching. The purpose of that proclamation is to get people into relationships with one another through micro-communities, where they can share their life of faith with one another as they seek to make love the goal of their lives. Here is where it all comes together: as people grow in their experience of God's presence and love moving in their lives, it is crucial that that love is shared outside of the group, outside of the traditional form of the church, through relationships that cross human-created boundaries that otherwise divide us. In so doing, not only do we directly follow the teachings of Jesus but we also encounter God's grace afresh and prevent our experience of faith from being focused on our own needs and ourselves.

Social Engagement Today

While encountering needs in Wesley's day was easy, societal structures today seek to insulate us from one another. We must begin with relationships. Consider an organization or community that you or your congregation is already in relationship with. Consider deepening that relationship through spending time with staff or constituents. Share a meal, invite people to share stories about where they are seeing hope and promise and about where they are encountering need. Invite them to share what brings them joy and helps their community come alive. Ask what the members of that community or organization wish they could do in order to make a greater impact through their work. Engage in prompts like these and other questions that might draw out commonality and a spirit of hopefulness.

As you listen—and make sure you do—consider how you can engage the relationship more deeply for the sake of sharing God's love. One of the most galvanizing and timely mission ministries that my (Chris) congregation is currently engaged in began with an invitation. The church had been without a chair of its mission committee since the beginning of the COVID-19 pandemic and was still languishing without one three years later. When a person with a significant background in humanitarian ministry joined our church community, a member of my team decided to ask him if he would be interested in leading the mission committee. He invited the team member who asked him and myself out to lunch to discuss the possibility. Ultimately he agreed to lead as long as he could bring his professional work and passion into the role and the ministry of our church: refugee resettlement—to which we gave him a resounding yes!

It wasn't long before we began to welcome new people to worship who had come to the US as asylum seekers. After some time, he followed up and asked if our congregation would be willing to resettle a family who had been officially granted refugee status by the US government. Not knowing all that it entailed, I immediately said that if the team would support his efforts, we should do it. By Christmas we welcomed a family with a team of over 30 people who did the necessary preparatory work of finding and furnishing an apartment, setting up a system of transportation, as well as surrounding them with the necessary support to enroll their children in school, take English classes, and ultimately find work. If someone had asked me a year prior if our congregation would have this work as one of our primary areas of mission focus, I would not have thought it would be likely.

The fact of the matter is that we kept saying yes to the spirit, and God provided. It was more a process of permission-giving than of missional discernment. Other people had the experience, vision, and calling to love our neighbors in this way. Almost all of the people who were a part of the resettlement team also belong to a micro-community such as a Grace Group or other form of small group. Again, the love that flows inward in faithful relationships also flows outward to build relationships across boundaries for the sake of Christ's mission.

Social engagement in your setting, church, or community could include anything that helps you to love your neighbor, which first requires you to know your neighbor. Challenge your small group, Grace Group, or whatever micro-communities that are in your church to engage social needs through boundary-crossing relationships as you keep the flow of God's love moving. Whether your group volunteers in renovating a home that will be sold at a low cost to people in need, as I did with my young adult pilot group at "Simple Homes" in North Philadelphia, or you encourage individuals to volunteer on their own, it is imperative to allow God's love to spin outward for the sake of the mission.

Befriend Your Neighbor

To practice the love of neighbor as Jesus teaches requires tangible action. We can certainly pray for others near and far, but to truly love our neighbor we must consider the same question that the lawyer asked Jesus in Luke 10:29: "Who is my neighbor?" Jesus answered the question by telling the parable of the good Samaritan. At the end of the story he asked the lawyer, who was the neighbor to the man on the side of the road. The lawyer's response: "the one who showed mercy." To be a neighbor is to show mercy, compassion, and love. But first, let us examine our neighborhoods.

I have to confess that like so many others today, I don't really know my neighbors. I see them take out the garbage, bring their kids home from school, walk the dog, get the mail, but I don't know most of their names, or anything about them. Many of them are newer to the area and we simply haven't had the opportunity to get acquainted. The truth is that too often the church functions the same way as the modern family. We think we know our neighbors and neighborhoods, but they have changed over time and the church doesn't always reflect the community that surrounds it. To harness the power of love spinning outward toward our neighbor we would do well to let go of toxic forms of charity that view that the people with means give money and possessions to people with lesser means. Instead, we embrace the call to get to know our neighbors, befriend them, walk with them, and find an encounter with the living God across boundaries and dividing lines through mutual service and the work of seeking justice and peace.

The traditional "mission" approach to addressing needs often identifies needs, areas, or populations of people who are in need and then seeks to fulfill those needs through collections, volunteer service, and other forms of support. However, keeping in mind that the Practical Quad is about the dynamic flow of love from element to element, we harness the love expressed and shared in micro-communities to then be directed outward toward others. This doesn't mean that a small group takes up a collection, but rather that members of the micro-communities get serious about loving their neighbors, whoever and wherever they are both as a group and individually. So we turn to the people around us, outside the walls of the church and in our towns, neighboring towns and places where we live our lives. The work begins with meeting and befriending our neighbors.

To befriend our neighbors and neighborhoods we offer a simple framework:

1. Listen
2. Foster Relationships
3. Assess Mutual Needs/Gifts
4. Tap into a Spirit of Abundance and Share

Listen

There is a well-worn image reinforced in culture of good neighbors taking a freshly baked pie to the family who recently moves in across the street. I don't know if this was ever truly the standard practice in most neighborhoods, but it has been in enough movies, books, and shows that it is ingrained in my imagination. The days of neighborly pies may be gone, but more than that, we too often aren't aware when people move out or in. Loving our neighbors requires that we pay attention with intention. Pay attention to the people who live, work, and spend time around you. Whoever they are there are two irrefutable truths about them:

1. They have been created and fashioned by the creator and are a beloved child of God.
2. They are worthy of receiving love.

Every person we meet has both gifts and needs. Loving our neighbor isn't just about giving money to the poor, but it is about forging relationships in which generous sharing can take place. So this begs the question, how can we befriend people we don't know? The first step is to listen. Engage a spirit of curiosity when interacting with people at local businesses, at community events, and with the people you meet in your community. Be curious about who they are, what they do, what are their hopes and challenges, what are their gifts, and what are their needs. Ask questions and listen.

This same principle is important when working with partner organizations as well. Instead of just donating money to local nonprofits that address the effects of poverty, take time to visit the organization, learn people's names, find ways to form a relationship with the people involved so that the partnership is built upon relationship rather than transactions between donor and receiver. And again, listen. Listen to what the highlights are, where people find hope, and what gifts and needs they have. When we ask people to share their stories we find commonalities that form the foundation of meaningful relationships.

Foster Relationships

I (Chris) recently approached a pastor that I deeply respect who works with vulnerable populations in a setting different from my own. When I asked him how my church could partner with his ministry he said, "Let's get lunch!" Instead of giving me a list of needs that I would then try to fill, he wanted us to get to know each other. Over tacos we shared our stories and he shared the pain of many suburban churches falling in the trap of playing "white savior" to the community in which he lives, only to disappear when the needs seemed to be too great, or when another project became more interesting. He wanted me to know the history, and to understand that his community had gifts and blessings, not just needs. He didn't want my charity. He wanted to foster a relationship.

Take time to attend events in communities in which you seek to serve, or consistently get together or communicate with them as you would a friend. Over time the fostering of relationships across the boundaries of socioeconomics, race, culture, and geography lay the groundwork for amazing and unexpected partnerships. It is here, in the context of relationships, that abundant sharing can happen.

Assess Mutual Needs/Gifts

Just over ten years ago the church I serve joined two other congregations and responded to an invitation to send a work team to the Los Cocos region of the Dominican Republic to build houses for families who were not able to afford their own homes. Each church would donate money for the supplies needed for the homes along with the volunteers who would serve along with Dominican carpenters as the construction crew. Now, after a decade, there are hundreds of houses in and beyond that village that have become a witness to the relationship built on mutuality that was formed between a group of American United Methodists and a Catholic family in the Dominican Republic who owned a construction company.

When the three churches originally answered the invitation to send teams to the Dominican Republic they assessed both the needs and the gifts that were presented. The gifts that were offered from the new partners in the Dominican Republic were the gifts of hospitality, deep spirituality, love for the most vulnerable in their local community, and most importantly, skilled labor. The partners in the Dominican Republic would open up their homes where the volunteers could stay while they were there, also providing community meals. The teams would go to church (Roman Catholic Mass) with their hosts and would welcome them into daily times of prayer and devotion. The central part of the partnership, however, was that the teams would raise money to hire professional crews to lay the foundation, install the load-bearing beams, and construct the roof so that the volunteers could build the walls and paint.

Over time the partner churches would receive guests from the villages to visit their churches in the US, providing hospitality and welcome. The guests often speak and share stories from the partnership in worship services and at church dinners. The missional partnership has turned into deep friendships, with people from both countries offering hospitality, time, and their different gifts for the purpose of providing basic housing for people who are in need. This past year our team returned from their work trip to report that many of the people who are living in homes built through the partnership are now giving back and volunteering to help build new homes.

When we befriend our neighbors, both near and far, it is important to assess our mutual gifts. People who live in economically disadvantaged regions and neighborhoods have gifts to offer. At the same time, people who benefit from greater resources and privilege have needs. In assessing what each party has to give and receive in the context of loving relationships, mutual sharing can transform the lives of all involved.

Tap into a Spirit of Abundance and Share

In 2012 when Superstorm Sandy hit the East Coast of the US, the town I (Chris) was living in at the time experienced a prolonged power outage due to hundreds of old trees being downed by powerful winds. The day before the storm was to make landfall I addressed people's fears of what was predicted to come and I told people from the pulpit in worship to be vigilant to care for their neighbors. For some reason, I was compelled to share in my benediction: if you or your neighbor loses power and the church still has it, our doors will be open and all are welcome to come, charge your devices, and stay warm.

Believe it or not, after hours of being pummeled with screeching winds, torrential downpour, and the sound of trees falling across roads and into houses, I drove to the church to find that it had power, even though almost every other section of town was without electricity. After posting on the church's social media pages that we had power and all were welcome, volunteers began to assemble to welcome people into the building so they could get warm and stay charged. Over the next 10 days our church would become a day shelter to up to 500 people a day who needed a place to work remotely, keep their kids entertained, charge their devices, and to get some food.

On the first day people started to ask if they could bring food from their refrigerators and freezers that were now thawing out at a rapid rate. A couple resourceful church members began cooking soups, stews, and other meals from the food that was being donated and serving it to the crowds that had gathered in our fellowship hall. Although the storm had done horrific damage in New York, New Jersey, and along the coast, something magical had happened in our church in the days that followed it. In the befriending of neighbors and mutual sharing of resources, deep inroads into the community and new relationships were formed. One of the members who was instrumental to the hospitality efforts in the church that week went on to work as a caseworker for people displaced by the storm through A Future with Hope, a nonprofit organization created by The UMC in New Jersey to manage the disaster response.

As God's love spins out through your micro-community and in your life, pay attention to the people around you—to laborers, to immigrants, to the people attending recovery groups in the church, to parents who are stretched too thin, to seniors who are feeling lonely, to people who are in need of tangible expressions of God's love—and befriend them. In listening, fostering relationships, assessing mutual gifts and needs, you can ultimately tap into a spirit of abundance and share with your neighbor. And, as I hear the teachers say to the kids in our church preschool on a daily basis, sharing is caring. Caring for your neighbor is loving your neighbor, as Jesus has commanded us.

Help Wanted!

"The size of the harvest is bigger than you can imagine, but there are few workers" (Matthew 9:37 CEB). Just as Jesus told his disciples, there is more work to be done for God's kingdom than there are workers, so we better train some new workers, and quick! If everything that we have laid out so far as ingredients of the Practical Quad seems like it will take a lot of work, you're not wrong. However, Wesley's genius was more than just his ability to preach to strangers outdoors, organize intricately woven communities and micro-communities, or marshal people into caring for the needs of others. Wesley's giftedness was also found in his ability to identify, recruit, equip, and commission leaders at every level from among the new people who came into the movement.

As we engage the hurts and needs of the world we will need new leaders who can listen to their neighbors, foster relationships, and assess the mutual gifts and needs among all parties involved. In order to sustain and multiply Wesley's dynamic method, we must adopt his rhythm for seeing leadership potential in people and activating them to serve as God has gifted them. But how can we develop new leaders when it seems like the pool for recruitment is constantly shrinking?

To help find ways to engage in missional relationships across boundaries for the sake of God's love, see the Social Engagement Guide on the following page.

Notes

1. John Wesley, *A Plain Account of Christian Perfection* (William Pine, 1753).
2. Richard P. Heitzenrater, *The Poor and the People Called Methodists* (Kingswood, 2002), 27.
3. Heitzenrater, *The Poor and the People Called Methodists*, 18
4. Heitzenrater, *The Poor and the People Called Methodists*, 18.
5. Heitzenrater, *The Poor and the People Called Methodists*, 21.
6. Heitzenrater, *The Poor and the People Called Methodists*, 27.
7. Heitzenrater, *The Poor and the People Called Methodists*, 27.
8. Heitzenrater, *The Poor and the People Called Methodists*, 28.
9. Heitzenrater, *The Poor and the People Called Methodists*, 33.
10. Heitzenrater, *The Poor and the People Called Methodists*, 34.
11. Heitzenrater, *The Poor and the People Called Methodists*, 37.

SOCIAL ENGAGEMENT

Building relationships across boundaries for mutual healing, wholeness, and justice-seeking

Love Your Neighbor

Take these steps to form mutual relationships where God's love can grow

1. ### Crossing Social Boundaries
Identify individuals or an organization from a different socio-economic, racial, cultural, or other social location in order to establish an authentic relationship in which love of neighbor can be embodied.

2. ### Mutuality
Engage in a relationship of mutuality, formed through listening to each other's stories, sharing and receiving each other's gifts, and identifying needs that can be met through mutual work.

3. ### Deep Solidarity
Cultivate deep solidarity by welcoming each other into community, share each other's stories, care for one another's hurts and needs, and allow the relationship to reshape and inform your own life.

Engage

Engage in mutual relationship across boundaries to seek justice, peace, healing, and wholeness

LEADERSHIP ACTIVATION

"Would anyone like to volunteer?"

"Blessed is the one who plants trees under whose branches they will never sit."
—*common proverb, origin unknown*

"Who among you is willing as well as able to supply their lack of service?"
—*John Wesley,* Plain Account of the Methodists[1]

> **Leadership Activation** is recognizing that everyone has gifts and graces from God that are ready and willing to be deployed in various roles and being willing to empower persons to use those gifts and graces.

The final element of the Practical Quad is Leadership Activation. Beyond leadership development or formation, leadership activation is a process of identifying, investing in, and deploying leaders to multiply the method that forms new disciples. As the early Methodist movement grew, there was a constant and growing need for new leaders at every level in order to multiply the societies, form new classes, and lead ministries of social engagement. Wesley commissioned circuit-riding preachers, class leaders, and different positions to lead each initiative to address social needs. But if Methodism was growing and many adherents were new to the movement, where would they find individuals who were seasoned enough to lead important leadership roles? Wesley's genius went beyond his abilities to organize networks, but was found in his distinct giftedness in identifying potential in new people and setting them loose for the sake of God's mission.

Today, a crisis of leadership is one of the many symptoms of church decline that can be experienced at every level from clergy to laity roles within a congregation. Many pastors and congregations have ideas of new programs or initiatives they would like to enact in order to reach new people, but too often the issue is that there aren't enough leaders to make an initiative viable. If churches are struggling to find new leaders to maintain current ministries and facilities, how can they ever recruit enough people to lead micro-communities and social engagement initiatives? The key is found in Wesley's method of leadership activation.

The Problem Today

By the twentieth century, The United Methodist Church had become the second largest mainline Protestant denomination in the United States, with over eighty autonomous and Wesleyan- or Methodist-related churches around the world. The massive growth of Methodism in a variety of forms occurred over time through multiplication in different countries, cultures, and languages. In biology, simple cells multiply more rapidly than complex cells. The method of the Wesleys and the early Methodists was rather simple and multiplicative. Field preachers took the message across England into Scotland and Ireland and ultimately to the American colonies. Everywhere the field preachers went they took a simple message of God's love for all, formed communities and micro-communities where people found belonging, and lived out their Christian witness by engaging the needs of others around them.

Just as the simplicity of Methodism led to its rapid multiplication, there is one last component that was essential to this growth: **leadership activation**. Without the practice of constantly identifying, equipping, and sending new leaders and preachers, Methodism would have remained as a community in either Bristol or London. Instead, early Methodists sought the potential in people, tapping them for leadership and setting them loose. This practice became a defining element to Methodism.

Jesus said that his disciples (which includes all of us who seek to follow Jesus today) are the salt of the earth. If salt loses its saltiness, it is no longer of use. Here's the thing about salt—it always eventually loses its saltiness after it has been used. You always need new salt! I grew up with snowy Northeast winters, which require that every household has a lot of salt. The thing about salting the sidewalks is that you need to keep doing it, especially if precipitation and freezing continue, which they often do over the course of several months. I'm always happy when I get to put the salt in the garage for the winter because it gets tracked into the house and can damage wood and clothing—because it is powerful.

Just as you always need to keep putting fresh salt out when it snows or freezes, the world will always need fresh salt. Generations of the faithful come and go. There will always be the need to proclaim good news to the poor and release to the captives. There will always be a need to sow seeds of love and to seek justice and peace in a world dominated by greed, fear, violence, and injustice. The world will always need new salt laid afresh in every generation. If we do not mine the salt within our own communities, who will?

The History

Early Methodist Leaders

If early Methodists were anything, they were salty. Puns aside, early Methodists were willing to step up when asked to assume a leadership role. Today we might want to cower in the corner and hope no one sees us when someone asks, "Can I get a volunteer for this?" But early Methodists were honored to fulfill a role when asked. It meant that their preacher (perhaps even John) saw the Spirit of God moving in them in a unique way. Before diving into the particularities of the types of leaders John developed, let's spend a minute and talk about a few concrete examples of whom Wesley empowered. A lot of laymen were given the basic leadership roles dictated below, but as someone who likes to uplift other women, I want to expound upon a couple of badass Methodist women whom John asked to serve in places of authority when society had cast them aside.

The first was Sarah Ryan. She was the daughter of an alcoholic and was forced into domestic servitude at a young age to try to bring some income to the family. Sarah was married three times. Her first husband, it turned out, was already married to another woman. Her second was maybe or maybe not an official marriage; intent to marry was declared but nothing beyond that. Her third marriage was to an Irish seafarer who eventually became very abusive, but he died at sea.[2] Side note for those who are not familiar with gender history: until the 1970s (yes 1970s, that is not a typo) women did not legally exist outside of a man. Through the legal doctrine of "coverture" women were either legally attached to their father or their husband. So when Sarah's husband died at sea (and her father had died by then too), she was left without a legal identity and therefore no name, no income, no existence.

Sarah had been a member of a Methodist society at the Foundery, brought there under the illustrious preaching of Whitefield. However, by 1754, she had turned her spiritual care to John Wesley and was assured. She wrote,

> I felt a cold sweat and a trembling come over me. . . . I felt my strength quite taken away, and fell out of my chair. In a moment I saw (not with my bodily eyes) the Lord Jesus standing before me and saying "This day is salvation come to this house." I saw all my works and attainments laid at his feet, as nothing worth: and I saw my soul, as it were, taken up and plunged into God. . . . [The Lord said] "Neither heights, nor depths, nor things present, nor things to come, nor any other creature, shall for one moment separate thy soul from me, in time or eternity."[3]

John wanted to help Sarah continue this new start in life and so he sent her to Bristol and gave her the role of housekeeper of the New Room. Again, side note: housekeeper in the eighteenth century is best thought of as a manager, and again remember, the New Room was the home base of Methodism. So this was a big gig! John tasked her with ensuring that all the activities in the New Room were worthy of the love of God, with ensuring that no "unprofitable conversation" occurred, and to ward off any "impertinent" visitors. She was to ensure that traveling preachers were cared for when they visited as well as to look after the teachers of Kingswood School (the Methodist school for colliers' children). A few years into her role as housekeeper she recorded her joy in the role:

> I now know where my strength lieth, and my soul is continually sinking more and more into God. I find my whole heart and affections entirely fixed on the Lord Jesus, I have no will but what is conformable to his; no happiness, but in doing his pleasure. . . . To him I entirely consecrate myself: to him be might, majesty, and dominion, now and for evermore![4]

When her health began to fail from stress, she joined Sarah Crosby and Mary Bosanquet in leading a house for destitute women and children called "the Cedars." They provided housing, education, food, and clothing to 35 children and 34 adults.

The second woman worth mentioning was also named Sarah (Crosby), and had also been married, abused, and abandoned by her husband. She heard John Wesley preach in 1749 and also joined the Foundery. Within a few years she began leading a class meeting. She, along with Mary Bosanquet and Sarah Ryan, began the aforementioned Cedars. However, Sarah Crosby felt a deeper call to preach than to attend to needs. By 1761 she was openly preaching and establishing new class meetings. Side note: it was very much against the rules of the Anglican Church (and most other sects or religions) at the time for women to preach. But Sarah never asked permission; the Spirit of God called her to preach, so she did. She did confess her preaching to John afterward, but he never explicitly told her not to preach. He advised how she might proceed forward by doing the things of a preacher but not referring to herself with such a title. Within the decade, however, John was openly acknowledging that the Spirit of God works in each of us in different ways, and that in Sarah Crosby it called her to preach.

I share these two illustrations to illustrate that John was not looking for just anyone to take on roles. He carefully looked at different gifts and graces of God within each person and saw that God called them to different leadership roles through those gifts and graces. I'll admit that even though I'm a do-er, I also hide in the corner when someone asks for a volunteer. I have too many of my own ideas and obligations to be asked by someone else to do something that I don't fully understand the purpose of. What we need to realize is that God truly does work in mysterious ways and sometimes God calls us to new ministries, new roles, new experiences of the Spirit through the question, "Would you like to volunteer for this?"

New Problems Activate New Leaders

As Methodism developed, new problems emerged. With each new problem, John didn't assume immediate control and try to fix it himself. He looked around at people's gifts and graces and created new places and spaces for them to become leaders. These new categories of leadership activation included class leaders, assistants, stewards, visitors of the sick, and schoolmasters. Leadership activation, for John, relied upon a desire to "serve their brethren in love."[5]

The Class Leader

One of the first places that John identifies a new leadership category was *the class leader*. Now remember, classes were developed originally to pay off the debt of the New Room and to collect tithes to address needs of the whole connection. These groups of people, at first, didn't actually gather together. Instead, it was more of a one-on-one with the class leader where each person was individually checked upon and their tithe collected. The duty of a class leader included "mak[ing] a particular inquiry into the behaviors of those whom he saw weekly." In laying out the specific duties of a class leader they were asked:

> To see each person in his class once a week at the least; in order to inquire how their souls prosper
>
> To advise, reprove, comfort, or exhort as occasion may require
>
> To receive what they are willing to give toward the relief of the poor
>
> To meet the Minister and the stewards of the society in order to inform the minister of any that are sick, or of any that are disorderly and will not be reproved

To pay the stewards what they have received of their several classes in the week preceding[6]

After asking class leaders to do all of the above, John soon realized (by being told by the class leaders) that this was way too much for one person to accomplish with a group of ten to twelve people. Visiting each person within their own home took too much time. Some people were not comfortable letting the class leader inside their home; oftentimes, they did not want to be known associating with "the Methodists." When a class leader was allowed inside, it was usually in a room full of people, which isn't exactly a great place to inquire about the deep state of one's soul. And, surprise, surprise: it seemed that when some people shared concerns about another person's salvific journey, the other might disagree. To address this problem, John encouraged the class leader to gather everyone together in one room, and address all their problems. This engagement benefited by creating another space (as discussed in chapter 2) where people could come together and grow in salvation together. But it also relieved the class leaders from potential burnout.

The Assistant

When the minister or preacher was absent, John asked that the assistant step in. It is very important to remember here that the assistant was usually a layperson. Their duties were plentiful, including:

To expound every morning and evening

To meet the United Society, the Bands, and Select Society, and the Penitents each week

To visit the Classes (London and Bristol excepted) once a month

To hear and decide all differences

To put the disorderly back on trial, and to receive on trials for the Bands or Society

To see that the Stewards, the Leaders, and the schoolmasters faithfully discharge their several offices

> To meet the Leaders of the Bands and Classes weekly, and the Stewards, and to overlook their accounts[7]

The above was no small task (and honestly reads quite like the typical week of a modern-day clergyperson). While these were the many duties of the assistants, they were expected to follow even more rules (ten rules in fact), but don't worry I won't list them all. They were expected to be diligent, serious, assume goodness of all persons, speak no evil, be honest with others, to not collect a personal paycheck or donation from persons, and to live out the gospel above all else. Again, seems very similar to our modern-day clergyperson. Assume the best; plan for the worst.

The Steward

As Methodism grew, as classes grew, so did the tithes. What a great problem to have! Tithes were collected weekly and were combined and then redistributed to meet the diverse needs of the community. However, this became too large of a job for the assistant or class leader to do well. And so, to address this problem, John created the steward whose business was:

> To manage the temporal things of the Society
>
> To receive the subscriptions and contributions
>
> To expend what is needful from time to time
>
> To send relief to the poor
>
> To keep an exact account of all receipts and expenses
>
> To inform the Minister if any of the rules of the society are not punctually observed
>
> To tell the Assistants in love if they think anything amiss, either in their doctrine or life[8]

They, too, had rules to follow along with the above duties. They were expected to be frugal, to take on no debt, to not have long accounts, to not judge persons whom they helped, and to not expect thanks from anyone. The stewards would gather together weekly and conduct their business, with the idea being that all tithes collected on a Tuesday were distributed to those in need by Thursday of that same week. However, while collecting tithes, the stewards began to notice that some persons "were ready to perish before they knew of their illness." And anyone who has been tasked with fundraising knows that you need to collect before an illness takes over. But being a steward, they were not delegated to provide medical or spiritual care, and thus "when they did know, it was not in their power (being persons generally employed in trade) to visit them so often as they desired."⁹ And thus, John responded and created the visitor of the sick.

The Visitor of the Sick

For this one, instead of creating a new category of leader and asking it to be filled, Wesley turned to the leaders and asked them to identify, among their class, someone who would be dedicated to visiting the sick. Their business was to include:

> To see every sick person within his district thrice a week
>
> To inquire into the state of their souls, and advise them, as occasion may require
>
> To inquire into their disorders and procure advice for them
>
> To relieve them, if they are in want
>
> To do anything for them which he (or she) can do
>
> To bring in his accounts weekly to the Stewards

Listening to the needs of these visitors prompted John to write the Primitive Physick as a tool, meant not only for persons to create their own remedies but also for visitors to be more able to assist those who were ill.

Why the History Matters

I'm sure if you've made it this far into this chapter and you're in a leadership role at the church, you may be thinking by now, "Sure, people in the eighteenth century were willing to volunteer their time because they had time." I myself am pretty bad at delegating. It's not for lack of trust;

it's more for a lack of patience. I'd rather just overwhelm myself than trust that others will get it done by the time it needs to be done. John, despite being a control freak, excelled at delegation. He had to! If he was going to be itinerant and focus on spreading Methodism, he couldn't afford to not trust others to continue the work of tending to souls.

Leadership activation provided John and his preachers with much-needed assistance and showed how adaptive Methodists were (and can be!) to problems as they arose. Today, do we delegate in the same way? Do we trust that others around us can handle responding to specific problems?

As a layperson, I don't think that we do. In early Methodism, both in John's day and in the first century of The Methodist Episcopal Church, the majority of leadership from day-to-day and week-to-week was done by the laity. Circuit riders and preachers itinerated, which meant that they were constantly moving, traveling from one town to another, often on a circuit of two hundred miles. A class or society would see them once every three months at best. Between the preacher's visits, the laity were the ones who kept the movement going and growing. It was them who stepped up and assumed the positions of exhorter, of class leader, of steward, of visitor of the sick, and so many other roles as new needs arose. As a layperson, today, one of the spaces where we have to do better in order to truly reclaim the method of Methodism is in empowering laity. And we can't simply turn over duties, but we have to ensure that laity are trained, educated, and know what they are doing, why they are doing it, and how to respond and lead in a truly Wesleyan and Methodist way. There has to be a more intentional training of laity that is readily accessible.

But also, we, as laity, have to allow the clergy to delegate to us. We cannot expect clergy to do *everything*. It's actually quite easy to pinpoint the moment in our past when laity became over-reliant upon clergy to lead. Once the circuits became smaller, as clergy married and established families, they began to settle into a community. As they settled *they* became *the* person someone went to for guidance; *they* became *the* person expected to visit the sick; *they* became *the* person expected to collect and distribute tithes; and *they* became *the* person responsible for ensuring that the flock continued to grow in salvation. Laity were slowly cast to the side—often pushed into the role of Sunday school teachers. However, over the last two decades, Sunday schools have become a thing of the past. So now where do laity go for a leadership role in the church where they are actively nurturing other disciples? I'm legitimately asking because I honestly do not know.

Without laity to rely upon and take some of the pressure off of attending to an entire congregation, clergy have become burned out at a rapidly increasing rate. As attendance has decreased so have budgets. As budgets have decreased so have staff. As staff have decreased so has programming. And as programming decreased so has attendance. It is a vicious cycle that essentially relies upon one clergy (maybe two if you're a larger church) to undo that cycle by increasing programming in order to increase attendance, which would hopefully increase budgets so that you can afford more staff. None of this is needed. If we intentionally activate leaders, taking into account their specific gifts and graces, disciples are nurtured in new ways.

While descendants of the Methodist tradition have helped to transform the world through education, health care, social reform, and the work of ministry over three centuries, the current state of Methodist institutions is in decline, particularly in Great Britain and the United States. The number of young clergy coming from both the British Methodist and United Methodist churches is at an all-time low, all while the average age of both denominations continues to rise. Spreading salt into the world to be a balm for the wounds and brokenness of society is not a one-time function, but a cycle that must be repeated and renewed from generation to generation.

Of course, the primary concern is not all about numbers. Much focus on declining numbers and metrics, and particularly how we can turn them around, has wearied many in church leadership, not least among them the authors of this book. However, every number represents a real person. When people leave and the number goes down, there is a real person who may feel displaced or disillusioned that the Christian church is not a place where they feel welcomed, or that The UMC is not a place that helps them connect to a living God. Numbers aren't the goal, but people are. And as we lose people who die, I give God thanks for their witness but grieve that we don't have the leaders coming up that can carry the torch of the saints who marched for civil rights, worked for justice, embodied love, and helped make the witness of Jesus Christ visible in this world. I grieve that at times it seems that the storms of life are heavier and the salt seems more scarce than it has ever been. Jesus said the work is plentiful, but the laborers are few. I have hope for our future, but the reality of that hope depends on our ability to build up the next generation of leaders.

When I try to explain to people within the church the importance of building up new leaders for the sake of continuing the church's mission beyond our lifetime, I think of an experience I had in my first job in college. During my freshman year, I began working at a pizza chain as a cook and delivery person. I remember distinctly that two days out of the year were uniquely crazy for pizza places: New Year's Eve and Super Bowl Sunday. On both days I remember a steady but manageable start to the shift. Calls would come in every few minutes and we were fulfilling orders and sending them out the door at short intervals. Then, all of a sudden the demand would increase to an unmanageable pace where we had to put multiple people on hold to take the orders on several different phone lines. The counters were overflowing with boxes and pans ready for pizzas to be made and then cut. After the surge, usually lasting one or two hours, business would slow down to a trickle over a few hours and eventually taper off. We wouldn't know when the night was over until orders stopped completely.

On those busy nights, I would watch the end of the pizza oven, which was a slowly moving conveyor belt that would fully bake a pizza in about eight minutes. There would be a steady stream of cooked pizzas coming through as long as someone started the process by making new pizzas and placing them into the oven. I watched for the last of the pizzas as we neared the end of a busy night, knowing that as long as we didn't get any new orders, the final pies of the evening would soon be baked and the night would be over.

While not a perfect analogy, there is something about the image of forming something new and waiting for it to mature, or in this case, bake, that helps me to think about the issue of leadership in the church. If we no longer are forming new leaders, or no longer calling young pastors, teaching children, or ministering to youth and young adults, it is a matter of time, and in some cases that time is already upon us, that the stream of faithful adults will come to an end. As our faithful church members, whose faith was formed in the twentieth century, age and pass away, there are fewer and fewer people to carry a message of unconditional love, to be salt and light for a hurting world.

While the task of attracting and forming faith among younger people is quite daunting, it is important to understand some systematic dysfunctions that have led to, or exacerbated, the current situation. While simple cells multiply rapidly, complex organisms struggle to replicate at a rate greater than attrition. The early models of Methodism were simple models that could be replicated without going through a formal hierarchy or power structure. If you had experience in a Methodist class meeting, you could start one yourself, as was the case with Barbara Heck in New York City in 1765. However, today, the complex processes, territorialism, and hierarchies that are often involved in church leadership can make attracting and engaging new people difficult and, frankly, discouraging.

In order to continue to meet new people where they are, beyond the walls of the church, to place them into micro-communities, and to empower them to engage social issues and justice concerns, new leadership is essential. But with aging structures, and people, how can the church build up new generations of leaders to be salt and light? Simply put, how can we make disciples of Jesus Christ for the transformation of the world? How can any method create new leaders among emerging generations that are increasingly nonreligious?

Build Up the Next Generation

In the spirit of Wesley and the Methodist movement, this model is not an intentional effort to recruit younger leaders. This is a method for cultivating a culture that taps and forms new leaders of all ages, generations, and social groups. It is about constantly teaching and empowering people to continually renew and multiply the work of God's kin-dom. Responding to Jesus's invitation to follow him and to make disciples invites us all to take our role in calling and equipping others seriously. We are all potential mentors, equippers, and disciple-makers. That is what it means to follow Jesus and to multiply his love in the world.

Staying true to John Wesley's theology and the practices of the early Methodist movement, leadership activation entails recognizing the divine image, or imago Dei, in each person and walking with them into becoming who God has created them to be. To see what people don't see in themselves—belovedness, gifts, leadership qualities, and potential—is ministry. But helping people to see their own gifts and divine imprint and nurture it into producing fruit for God's work of redemptive love takes work, patience, and faith.

Leadership Activation Framework

Activating new leaders for the sake of sharing God's love for the redemption of the world requires four crucial steps:

1. See God's image and giftedness in each person
2. Plant seeds
3. Invest in people
4. Set them loose

See God's Image (Imago Dei)

Understanding the importance of seeing the divine image in others, even when they don't see it in themselves, is something deeply personal for me and central to my own faith story. As a child who wasn't allowed to miss a week of church or Sunday school, I often struggled to sit still, pay attention, or follow the rules. I was a kid with ADHD in the 1980s, when it was not commonly recognized as something to be accommodated, and kids who couldn't sit still were punished for being bad in school and church. There were weeks where I was asked by the teachers to leave Sunday school early and go find my parents because of my behavior. I distinctly remember an encounter with a very short, older lady named Mrs. Sheckler, who I guessed at the time must have been about 130 years old, coming over to me as I hid outside of the sanctuary after I was kicked out of Sunday school. Mrs. Sheckler said to me, "Chris, do you know how special you are?" To which my internal monologue replied, "Do you know how crazy you are?" She continued, "You are a very special young man. God is going to do something special with you."

Of all of the amazing people in my life who taught, mentored, and supported me along my faith journey and pathway into ordained ministry, I am certain that if Mrs. Sheckler had not spoken to me the way she did, I would probably not still be in the church. Over the years of my adolescence, she would continue to encourage me, show me the piano, tell me stories about the stained glass windows, and show me love as though I was someone very special. She didn't care that I got in trouble, and didn't listen to the people who complained about my inability to self-regulate. She saw something in me, deep within, that others didn't see and I certainly couldn't see in myself. She saw the image of God within me and told me about it. Her speaking of and about me in this way changed my life and planted the seed, the idea that perhaps God did love me and could work through someone like me.

I believe that because of Mrs. Sheckler's ability to see beauty in a misbehaving kid, I have held throughout my own ministry the value of seeing beauty within people despite their brokenness. Being able to see gifts within people even when they struggle to have faith, or wrestle with addiction or family relationships, or have difficult personalities. God has made and dwells within every human heart. Each person who is entrusted to us in community needs others to see and reflect back to them their belovedness, and to remind them that God has given them gifts to share.

In order to activate leaders for the sake of sharing God's liberating love, we must first look deep into the people within our micro-communities and see how God is present and moving to redeem their brokenness. When we listen to people share, thank them for their honesty and vulnerability, and remind them of their belovedness, we can help people begin to see their own divine image, or *imago Dei*, which will become more visible as they grow in living out their faith through service.

Plant Seeds

One of the unhealthy patterns of leadership that I have encountered throughout my ministry is leadership squatting. It is when someone takes on an area or role of leadership and doesn't share it, but holds it indefinitely until they can no longer serve or they die. I can't even recall how many good people in churches squat in leadership roles unwilling to teach, mentor, or shepherd others in leadership out of fear of losing the power that their particular role or area of ministry gives them. It is good as long as they perform the role well and for the right reasons, but inevitably when leadership squatters die or leave the church without mentoring a successor, the ministry dies, or is thrown into chaos as important institutional memory is lost.

In stark comparison is a phrase I learned from my physician wife that is often used within the medical community among trainees like medical students and residents: "see one, do one, teach one." This saying indicates a cycle and culture of constantly learning, doing, and teaching. The first time a medical student sees a medical procedure, they watch for the purpose of learning, knowing that soon they will have to do it with supervision and then independently. Particularly, the phrase conveys the understanding that students will soon become residents who will become attending physicians and teachers, and that they will continue to learn new skills in a repeating cycle of learning, growing, and passing along knowledge and experience. It changes how we do things when we know we are expected to teach others, which requires a willingness to let go and trust others to do. In a culture of "see one, do one, teach one," you can't get too calcified in a role, but instead see yourself as a constantly growing and evolving part of a greater ecosystem of learning.

Planting seeds of leadership in people means to constantly keep the ecosystem open, including and inviting new people to be a part of whatever you are doing. Even in a closed Grace Group, make sure you are including people who are not already involved in a bunch of other places in ministry. Continually create opportunities for new people to not only become a part of the community but to take ownership of things both great and small. Within the 12-step recovery community, there are all kinds of service positions to ensure that new and seasoned people can always serve. For someone who is brand new to the recovery journey, making coffee or setting up chairs can be a really big deal. Having something positive to contribute and having the trust of the community is a crucial entry-level step to feeling welcomed and important to the community. In the same vein, it is central to constantly welcome new people into the space and give them something to do. Remember that as people of faith, we too should always be thinking about growing and leading others in growth. "See one, do one, teach one" should be the church's motto for discipleship.

Invest in People

When you plant seeds outside, you should do it at the right time in the correct season so that they get the water and sunlight needed to grow. If you plant seeds in a pot, you need to make sure that you water them yourself with the appropriate amount and timing. In the same way, when we see the divine potential in people and invite them into community through service, it is important to invest in people to ensure they have the support, mentoring, and relationships necessary to flourish. Churches are great at dropping people into committees and new leadership roles without any support or preparation only to be surprised when the person doesn't stick around. If you want a seed to grow, you have to nurture it.

I have been in both positions in my life: in over my head without a lifeline, and supported by good mentors who invested in me. While I can write a book about the times when I felt like I was drowning without proper support, the truth is that there have been many incredible people—laity and clergy—who initiated and sustained relationships with me that made all the difference. One of those people for whom I'm deeply grateful is Brian. Brian is a pastor in my conference and has chosen of his own volition to Zoom with me once a month to support my ministry. This mentoring relationship began early on in the pandemic when I was struggling to keep it together, as each day required a new pivot along with more anxiety and grief. Brian said that he wanted to "pour into me" as a way to support my pastoral leadership and invest time in me. Instead of trying to fill me up with knowledge or information, Brian poured time, curiosity, empathy, and hope into me. His main approach was to listen to me about anything and everything. Each time we meet Brian asks, "What would be helpful today?" I usually ramble until I pinpoint the quandary that I realize I could use feedback on or a problem that I could use a listening ear to work through. It was only recently, when we went a month without our regular call, that I realized how much his investment in me has meant. Brian was one of the earliest and strongest cheerleaders for this book project.

How many younger and new people within our communities and churches could use people to check in on them and support them in their life of faith? Even having coffee once a month or checking in on the phone or Zoom on a regular basis can make a tremendous difference over time. Just like watering plants, we don't necessarily see the results of our efforts until we can look back over time. And yet, if you want to know just how important nurturing a plant is, try not watering it for a couple weeks. You will see the negative results quickly. In this spirit I have begun to regularly check in with some of the young adults from my pilot Grace Group to see how they are doing, to listen to them and ask how I can support them or pray for them. If efforts like this were to become a defining characteristic of how we grow new disciples and leaders, just imagine what the results could look like over time.

Set Them Loose

In order for a cell to multiply, it must first divide. The two halves of a divided cell become two cells. In the same way, multiplication models of leadership ultimately require separation from the original group or cell. As long as Jesus was still around, the group of twelve disciples were dependent upon him for their leadership and identity. It was only after the Crucifixion and Resurrection that the disciples ultimately began to multiply the movement by making other disciples. But first, they needed to be set loose to lead.

My first appointment as a licensed local pastor was intended to be pulpit supply, whereby I was only to preach and lead worship for a few months for a pastor who was on leave battling cancer. Fresh out of seminary, I was eager to lead the church by myself. On my first day of the job, I was informed that the pastor had unfortunately passed away that morning. Deeply saddened for the church and the pastor's family, I was hesitant to be thrust into the role of "pastor" so quickly and in such sad circumstances. That evening the district superintendent took me to dinner and assured me that the people needed my care and leadership more now than before. "But what am I supposed to do?" I asked him. "Your job is simple," he said, "love the people."

Perhaps "love the people" is a well-worn cliché that clergy tell one another about the role of pastor, yet I have held onto that conversation for over twenty years in ministry. When I literally felt like I was being dropped into the middle of the ocean with nothing to keep me afloat, the DS had given me a lifeline. He reminded me to let love be the center and the guide. With the idea of "love the people" as my true north, I jumped into the waters and God did beautiful things to help the people heal and find joy in the midst of sadness.

Multiplying leadership requires taking risks on people, understanding that it just might not work out, but it's worth it anyway. By seeing God's movement in unlikely people, giving them opportunities to serve and pouring into them, we come to the point where we need to let people swim on their own. Sometimes it's a nudge, or a gentle push into places and roles that people may not be entirely comfortable with but of which they are completely capable. To activate new leaders requires both you and the new leader to get out of your comfort zone for the sake of the mission. Take a risk, and let love be the goal, the guide, and the backup plan.

Leadership Activation Today

In terms of the Practical Quad, the last component is the most vital and most easily ignored. The church can engage in field preaching, micro-communities, and even social engagement for the sake of its mission, but to engage and activate new leaders can be a real challenge, as it requires people to take risks and share power. But when we can see activating new people in leadership as our own success and the formation of a healthy ecosystem of disciples making disciples for the purpose of putting out fresh salt into the old wounds of the world, we can find joy in it. But what does leadership activation look like today?

In the pilot Grace Group that I formed for my doctor of ministry project, I required all of the participants to take a post-project survey, which included a section on gifts and leadership assessment. The series of questions inquired of each member's sense of giftedness, interest, and calling to lead and serve in a variety of areas. I used the results to invite the different members into positions of leadership or service within ministry, including to co-lead a new Grace Group, serve on our pastoral visitation team, lead a monthly work team at a partner organization, and other roles.

Leadership activation in the Methodist spirit means to help people to find a role within the model to help move beyond the walls of the church with a message of love, to lead others into becoming a part of micro-community, or to engage in the work of social engagement and justice seeking. Each person has their own gifts, interests, and sense of calling, but it may take exposing them to different opportunities and encouraging them to try leading in order to help them grow into where God is calling them to be in that season. I often let different members of the Grace Group facilitate the meeting each week to let them see how it feels and to see if there is a giftedness that might become apparent to others as well.

Whether it is serving within or outside the church, our job as leaders in this model is to see the divine image in each of our people. We tend to the group dynamic as an open ecosystem where everyone has something to give and receive, something to teach and learn. We invest in one another, check in, spend time, communicate, and encourage. Ultimately, we take risks by setting people loose as new team leaders, field preachers, content creators, facilitators, visitors, and caregivers. It is truly only when we can multiply the leadership of field preaching, micro-communities, and social engagement that the model can replicate beyond church walls, offering a future with hope for the life-giving, both/and Wesleyan faith that our world needs. In the face of materialism, Christian nationalism, and the rejection of Christianity as a source of trauma and harm, we know that the gospel of Jesus Christ offers an alternative narrative. That alternative is God's unconditional, liberating love. All we need to do is set people free to multiply it in the world.

Mentoring New Leaders

The Practical Quad invites us to lean into the dynamic movement between field preaching, micro-communities, social engagement, and leadership activation, as God's love flows from one experience to the next. This engages people in the excitement and energy that comes from loving God and neighbor along with others. When activating leadership within new people, it is important to not just dump them into a job or role, but mentor them as they grow. While there are many great books on leadership and mentoring that go deeper on best practices, I suggest here a simple framework for mentoring people into new leadership roles:

1. Curiosity
2. Creativity
3. Courage
4. Care

Pay Attention to Curiosity

When I was in middle school, I mentioned to my mom one day that I thought I might want to be a pastor when I grew up. My mother's immediate response was to send me to tell the pastor of our church and see if he could advise me. It is worth noting that by middle school I did not present as the most likely candidate to pursue pastoral ministry. I struggled in school, got in trouble at church, and was trying to find my place among the other kids in youth group. When I reluctantly approached the pastor to share with him my big news (or so I thought) that I thought it might be possible that God wanted me to be a pastor, he gave me a puzzled look as though completely surprised not knowing what to say. After a moment of looking around his office he grabbed a very large brown biography of John Wesley and handed it to me. He said, "Here, go home and read this, then come back and we'll talk about it." This was not exactly the response I expected.

After the book sat on the top of my dresser for several months, my mother told me that if I wasn't going to read it, I had to return it to the pastor that week after church. When I handed him the book and thanked him for loaning it to, he asked, "What did you think of it?" "It was good," I said, and we never spoke of it again. While I have deep appreciation and admiration for that pastor today, and am proud to have had him as my pastor growing up, what I learned from my own experience is that when young people reveal their curiosity, pay attention!

As my mentor-friend, Brian, told me in response to my story, "People want you to give them yourself, not a book." Books are good, and books are important, but when people show that they are exploring something, or curious about learning more, tug at the curiosity and give them your time. Asking questions about people's hopes, dreams, fears, challenges, and sense of calling is a great start. When that person opens a door, walk through it. If they say, "I'd love to run a nonprofit organization to help people someday," follow up with your own curiosity and explore the possibilities of what they could do and who they might help if the sky was the limit. Dreaming together can deepen trust and deepen relationships.

Fuel Creativity

"The creative one"—this is a title I often received as a child, usually by teachers, friends' parents, and Sunday school teachers when they were trying to say something more positive than "he can't sit still or pay attention very well, can he?" The reality is that we are all creative beings. God, the creator, created us and that same energy to create is a part of the divine image within us. As we invest in people it is important to go beyond exploring their curiosity to fuel their creativity. For me as a kid with ADHD there was nothing that would make me love a teacher more than when they would let us be creative with learning projects—using experiences, technology, art, music, and invention to explore ideas.

In the same way, creating experiences for people to explore their curiosity can make all the difference between whether or not they live into their full leadership potential. Many years after my pastor loaned me the John Wesley book (I guess that one did pan out!), another pastor at the same church identified in me the call to ministry and created two very important opportunities that ultimately changed my life. He asked a family in the church if they would donate money to pay me a stipend to serve as the director of youth ministries—my first ministry job in the church. The second opportunity he created was that he asked the United Methodist Women if they would give me a scholarship to pay for my travel expenses to go on a mission trip to the Holy Land.

This pastor's resourcefulness went beyond encouraging me to pursue ministry and created experiences that would confirm my call to ministry and leave a lasting impression on me in the process. Investing in new leaders often requires just that: investing in them. Find scholarships, take people on trips, create experiences that expose them to new ideas, or send them to a conference that might open their eyes to what else is possible. Pay attention to a young person's curiosity and fuel their creativity.

Build Courage

Taking a leadership role in ministry, whether it is in leading a small group, organizing a mission experience, running a program, or pursuing pastoral ministry, requires courage. It is all too easy to doubt yourself, especially when working with people, and even more so when we are seen as representing our Christian faith community. We might not feel that we have enough faith, qualifications, or training, and yet when others put their trust in us, it is our job to lead. Therefore, mentoring people requires building up their courage. This goes beyond building up confidence. Confidence can be misplaced and easily shattered if we fail. Courage makes it possible to take risks knowing that God can use us even if we fail.

My church recently launched a drama ministry for children and youth to put on a major musical as a fundraiser for a new mission project. Among the many children who auditioned for the musical were my own two daughters, who auditioned in hopes of getting lead roles. I wasn't sure what to expect, as my younger daughter had not yet been in a play and my older daughter had never sung solo on a stage before. I was honestly bracing for the possibility that they wouldn't get the parts that they wanted, or worse, that they would get the parts but not put the work in to do as well as they wanted. After the auditions they were informed that they got the top roles that they each wanted. They were ecstatic.

As the months of rehearsals went on they wouldn't practice their vocal parts in front of me so I really didn't know how they were coming along. I knew that they had great acting abilities but again, I didn't know if they would put the work in to get the results that they wanted. By the time of the opening show, I was absolutely blown away with how great they did—how amazingly well all of the kids did. The experience of that musical taught each of the kids what they were capable of and gave them a vision for the future—to continue to act and sing, and work together. It certainly built confidence, but more than that it rewarded their courage to take risks with greater courage. Many of the kids went on to participate in musicals at their schools and most of them regularly ask about what musical the church will do next year. Fueling people's creativity builds up their courage, which will serve them well in leadership.

Take Care

The last element in this mentoring framework is often overlooked when investing in new leaders. However, we must take care with people if we want to model healthy and loving leadership.

A fellow graduate student shared a saying with me for which I have never been able to track down an attribution: "When teaching love, do so lovingly." The irony is that the church and other faith-based institutions often proclaim and teach love in ways that are anything but loving or caring. At the end of the day, people are people. They have faults, failures, things that go wrong, and things happen in their lives. Through the course of leadership people get sick, they lose loved ones, go through divorces or relationship fractures, lose jobs, have financial crises, and can struggle with their mental health.

As we pour into people and mentor them into leadership we must do so with a spirit of grace and above all, with care. When I was a young clergyperson in my twenties my grandmother, whom I loved very much, died. Within hours I received a phone call from my bishop, who prayed with me. Around the same time the senior pastor that I was working with at the time came by my house to pray with me in person. While they didn't have to respond as directly or as quickly as they did, their acts of care made a deep impact on me and helped me know that I was more than just an employee or pastoral staff person, but that I was cared for. Taking time to show care for the people you mentor and are activating as leaders will pay dividends over time. It builds trust, solidifies relationships, strengthens commitment, and can help people get through difficult seasons with the knowledge that they are not alone.

Activating the full leadership potential of people, young and old, new and seasoned, requires vision and investment. It takes seeing the divine image in each person, planting seeds of possibility in their lives, investing in them, and ultimately setting them loose. As leaders form, we continue to mentor and accompany them by paying attention to their curiosity, fueling their creativity, building up their courage, and taking care of them along the way. When we activate new leaders we develop capacity for growth by multiplication, which starts the Practical Quad over again.

Field preaching leads to micro-communities, which move people outward toward social engagement, which allows for leadership activation, which creates new field preachers, micro-community leaders, social engagement organizers, and mentors who activate new leaders. You get the point! The Practical Quad is a method, not a menu. It is the energy that flows from one element to the other that creates spirit movement and can transform the world one person at a time.

1. See God's Image and giftedness in each person
2. Plant Seeds
3. Invest in People
4. Set Them Loose

Notes

1. John Wesley, "The Character of a Methodist," *The Works of John Wesley: The Methodist Societies, History, Nature, and Design*, volume 9 (Abingdon Press, 1989).

2. Her third husband may have lived and ended up in America. All of this would make an excellent soap opera.

3. As quoted in G. M. Best, "Sarah Ryan: housekeeper at the new room and Kingswood school," accessed 2/13/25; https://www.newroombristol.org.uk/sarah-ryan/.

4. Best, "Sarah Ryan."

5. John Wesley, *A Plain Account of Christian Perfection* (William Pine, 1753).

6. Wesley, *Plain Account*, 261.

7. Wesley, *Plain Account*, 271.

8. Wesley, *Plain Account*, 273.

9. Wesley, *Plain Account*, 274.

CONCLUSION

How to employ the Practical Quad

"The distinguishing marks of a Methodist are not [their] opinions of any sort, [their] assenting to this or that scheme of religion, [their] embracing any particular set of notions. . . . A Methodist is . . . one who 'loves the Lord [their] God with all [their] heart, and with all [their] soul, and with all [their] mind, and with all [their] strength. . . . [They] are therefore happy in God . . . having in [them] 'a well of water springing up into everlasting life,' and overflowing [their] soul with peace and joy. Perfect love having now 'cast out fear,' [they] 'rejoice evermore.'" —John Wesley, 1742

Over the past 300 years, the legacy of the Methodist movement has left an incredible impact on the world in terms of spiritual revival, empowering marginalized people, addressing social and humanitarian problems, as well as addressing physical needs. Today as various Methodist-related institutions are in decline, there is much more than simply an organization on the line. Behind policies that enable unjust practices and unjust systems, as well as exploitation of marginalized people is too often bad theology, or a mistaken idea that, in the words of Howard Thurman, lift up the "religion about Jesus," instead of the "religion of Jesus." The primary difference between the two is that one makes belief in Jesus as God the primary goal, while the religion of Jesus takes the words of Jesus, and puts them into practice seriously. The theology of John Wesley, and the early Methodists, was developed around a vision of scriptural Christianity in which Christians were to first and foremost follow Jesus's teachings, and seek to put the love of God into practice in every area of their lives.

Today the world needs good theology, rooted in the grace and love of God more than ever. Too often a narrative prevails that religion is the root of the world's problems, including war, injustice, and the marginalizing of peoples. While it is true that spiritual malpractice has long been at the root of human corruption, the antidote for bad theology is not no theology, but theology, rooted in the heart of God, through the teachings of Jesus. Methodist theology claims first and foremost that God created people, and all of creation as good and beloved. While the divine image is hidden and obscured in the brokenness of the world, it is restored and reclaimed, as we live into the grace of God, and practice the unconditional love of God in the world. But this cannot be done in isolation. There is no holiness apart from social holiness.

The real challenge is that while we have this amazing message in clay jars, the methods the church has used for centuries is no longer yielding the fruit it once did. No amount of effort to double down on the traditional forms of worship or faith formation will magically make people flock into our buildings. There's too much on the line and there is too much at stake. The message must travel. We are at a tipping point, and must submit to be more vile, which means learning new methods, engaging, new technology, and going to uncharted waters for the sake of multiplying God's liberating love. We are at a critical moment where we must call on the fire of our origin. This book and its message is about passing on the flame of a movement rather than worshiping the ashes of a declining institution.

Reclaiming the method of methodism requires dynamic movement along the fourfold method of field preaching, micro-communities, social engagement, and leadership activation. First, the message must travel as we embark in new forms of field preaching. For many of us, that which is vile are the practices that we see flourishing today but seem foreign to the church. Showing gauge in field preaching in the twenty-first century includes engaging:

- Digital spaces
- Secular spaces

- Modern forms of technology and communication
- Creating art

In the spirit of early Methodism, preaching is not a destination in itself, but exists for the purpose of inviting people into relationships through micro-communities. Communities like Grace Groups can serve as alternatives to the many spaces that focus on debating opinions, theology, and politics, but rather tend one another's souls along the journey of faith. Creating small groups for the purpose of helping one another to experience and share the unconditional love of God can be both transformational and life changing. Wesley realized the need for something different from simply offering another study or curriculum based on the transfer of information and knowledge, Wesley and micro-communities put relationships at the center. In the midst of a loneliness epidemic and a decreasingly empathetic society, deeper relationships with God and one another is what people need the most.

But any community that is formed in our rapidly changing society today will ultimately shift in membership. If the focus is on maintaining the internal dynamic, it will inevitably decline. However, by engaging the hurts and needs of others outside of the group as a natural outflow of the love experienced within the micro-community, God's grace is strengthened and renewed among those involved. Engaging in relationships across human boundaries serves in direct obedience to the teachings and example of Jesus Christ. It is along the margins and pressures of life that sharing love, even when difficult and uncomfortable, has the power to transform lives, communities, and even the world.

Like any growing movement, new components require new leadership. The church doesn't need a new program for training leaders. We need a new culture in which people do not see positions as places to squat for power or position, but instead constantly see new people as worthwhile investments. The work of this model requires seeing God's image in each person, planting seeds, welcoming in their lives, investing in them by fostering relationships, and ultimately setting them loose, even when it is risky. By becoming an open ecosystem, where newcomers become doers who become teachers, who become mentors, we can multiply the method that delivers God's unconditional love to those who need it the most in our hurting world.

Where to Start?

Perhaps you are ready. You have come to the point where you know that something needs to change. You are tired or excited or both. You, like a young John Wesley in 1739, are ready to submit to be more vile. But what does that look like for you, in your context today? For Wesley, it was being invited to see and participate in something his friend was already doing but up to that point he was not willing to consider—preaching outside to working-class people in plain language so that they would understand the good news. The best place to begin is to evaluate the invitations or opportunities that have already been at your feet, but internal or institutional resistance has caused you or your people to decline to pursue. Maybe it is podcasting, coffee shop ministry, planting small groups in a brewery, or starting a Spanish-speaking ministry with the migrant community in your neighborhood. Consider the invitation of the spirit and follow it.

If you are still unclear, begin by forming a new micro-community with the intention of multiplying it by setting the members loose in a year or two. About a decade ago I (Chris) was having a conversation with UM pastor and author Rudy Rasmus about the church I was serving at the time. I shared with him both my love for my congregation and my frustration at not being able to shift the change-resistant culture that seemed deeply embedded within the leadership. I asked him, "Rudy, what would you do if you came here as pastor?" His answer irritated and ultimately inspired me: "Well, I'd do what Jesus did. I would identify eight to twelve people that I thought had the capacity for future leadership and put them into a group. I would invest in them, and help them grow in their faith and love of Jesus. And then, after a year or so, I'd ask them to split up and start several new groups where they do the same thing with others." Although intriguing, my defeated spirit immediately determined it was too simplistic and wouldn't work. I wanted to do it; I just didn't think I could find that many people who would commit to a group for that long.

Conclusion

It took me ten years and a church move until I actually took Rudy's advice. When I formed my first pilot Grace Group just two years ago, it was his vision that was in my mind. After leading a Grace Group of seven people for a couple years, I have personally witnessed the transformative power of this experience, not only on the group members, but on their families and on the church as a whole. The members of that group have each individually gone through a series of crises, serious challenges, and great blessings. Because of the strength of the micro-community, their ability to navigate difficult situations and to grow in their ability to experience and share God's love in the midst of it has been profound. That growth has spilled over to their families, their children, and into each of them stepping up to leadership in other spaces both within and outside of the church. We are now at the place where we are wrestling with the decision to split up and multiply, or to stay together as a group, as the relationships formed have become so life-giving. This fork in the road is a good problem to have and I'm sure God will give us the discernment we need to change when the time is right.

If you are not ready to go into the virtual field and preach online, or start a ministry in a secular space with strangers, perhaps you can begin by forming a new Grace Group that centers relationships rather than opinions—love over agreement on issues—and see what God can do over time. The most important thing, however, is motion. The elements of this method are not items on a menu. Too often the church focuses on small groups OR mission, OR worship, OR Christian education. Calling on the fire of the Methodist movement is about exactly that: MOVEMENT. Moving people along the experience of encountering God's love, embodying love in relationship, sharing love across boundaries, and then empowering new people to become ambassadors of that love. This is the Method—dynamic movement of God's grace beckoning people to experience and share the love of God with the neighbor, stranger, enemy, foreigner, sick, impoverished, and the imprisoned. By allowing God's grace to move through us in motion, we are transformed and the world along with us.

This book began with the claim that the church today has a mission without a method: to make disciples of Jesus Christ for the transformation of the world. But how? How can we participate in the formation of new disciples in an increasingly un-religious society too often dominated by toxic theology that excludes, limits, and condemns others without submitting itself to the radical love of Jesus? We believe that the method today is the same as it was in 1739. The same spirit fire that manifested in Bristol and emanated across the globe is available to us today if we can submit to be more vile and engage uncomfortable spaces and opportunities to:

1. Preach in new fields
2. Form new micro-communities
3. Engage the hurts and needs around us
4. Build up and activate the next generation of leaders

Not only do we believe in this historic method, but we are witnessing it bear fruit wherever it is practiced within Methodism as well as non-denominational and other denominational traditions. It is great to have open doors, but we don't have to wait for people to walk through them. Let us go and make disciples, channeling God's grace in motion to embody God's liberating love to a hurting world.

Put the Practical Quad into Practice

New ideas and theories are great. Benedictions are encouraging. Advice can be helpful. But so often we walk away from these pieces still asking: "so, what does this actually mean for me and how can I put it into practice in my own life?" Consider the four elements that we have proposed here: field preaching, micro-communities, social engagement, and leadership activation, and assess which of them, if any, are you already doing? Begin with the elements you have and explore how you might add another element to connect the flow of energy to create momentum working all of the elements of the Practical Quad together.

Perhaps your church has a food pantry or thrift store. If so, start there. Explore how you might connect serving there with small groups or a new Grace Group that you can form. Consider what field preaching would look like for your community, or the population you are seeking to connect with a message of God's liberating love. Perhaps you have two or three of the components of the Practical Quad already but they aren't connected together. If that is the case, connect your field preaching with real micro-communities where people can share their faith together. Connect small groups with your mission partners. Whatever the next step is, imagine that you are plugging in different elements to one another to channel a synergy of spiritual momentum. When God's love is proclaimed where people are, connects them in community with others, moves people beyond themselves to engage the needs and gifts of others, and forms new leaders, the true power of Method-ism can be harnessed.

Begin where you are with who you have in the setting in which you find yourself. Find one starting point and develop it. Connect each component with one another to walk people through the Wesleyan means of grace, which are conduits through which we experience the grace of God. Help people share their experience of God's grace working in their lives, and multiply it. What would you do to get unstuck and begin to make disciples of Jesus Christ for the transformation of the world? "I'd do what Jesus did. Start with a few willing people, help them grow in grace, and set them loose."

May it be so. **Amen.**

www.ingramcontent.com/pod-product-compliance
Lightning Source LLC
LaVergne TN
LVHW030242250326
834688LV00047B/1766